Winning the Heart of Your Stepchild

Other books by Robert Barnes

Ready for Responsibility
Who's In Charge Here?

with Rosemary Barnes

Great Sexpectations
Rock-Solid Marriage
We Need to Talk

Winning the Heart of Your Stepchild

Previously titled *You're Not My Daddy*

Dr. Bob Barnes

ZondervanPublishingHouse

Grand Rapids, Michigan

A Division of HarperCollinsPublishers

Winning the Heart of Your Stepchild
Copyright © 1992, 1997 by Robert G. Barnes, Jr.

First Zondervan edition, 1997

Previously published as *You're Not My Daddy: The Step-Parenting Process*

Requests for information should be addressed to:

📖 ZondervanPublishingHouse
Grand Rapids, Michigan 49530

Library of Congress Cataloging-in-Publication Data
Barnes, Robert G., 1947-
    [You're not my daddy]
    Winning the heart of your stepchild / Bob Barnes.
        p.   cm.
    Originally published : You're not my daddy. Dallas : Word Pub., c
1992.
    ISBN: 0-310-21804-7 (pbk.)
    1. Stepparents—United States.   2. Remarriage—United States.
3. Stepfamilies—United States.   4. Parent and child—United States.   I.
Title.
[HQ759.92.B37   1997]
306.874—dc21   97–3341
                                                                   CiP

All Scripture quotations, unless otherwise indicated, are taken from the
Holy Bible: New International Version®. NIV®. Copyright © 1973, 1978,
1984 by International Bible Society. Used by permission of Zondervan
Publishing House. All rights reserved.

Printed in the United States of America

97 98 99 00 01 02 03 04 /❖ DH/ 10 9 8 7 6 5 4 3 2 1

Contents

Acknowledgments   7
Introduction   9

Part 1
Before the Step-Parenting Begins

1   Before the Marriage Takes Place   13
2   The Guilt of the Child   20
3   Romancing the Child   30

Part 2
What's Happening to This New Family?

4   Am I Crazy or Is This Child Actually
     Trying to Sabotage Our Marriage?   37
5   The Child Lost More Than He Gained   45
6   Corporate Staff Meetings Are Mandatory   53
7   "Excuse Me, What Do I Call You?"   60
8   His, Hers, and Theirs   68
9   "It's Not Fair, and I'll Tell You Why"   75
10   But What If My Child Needs to
     Talk with Me Privately?   82

Part 3
Dealing with Behavior As a Team

11   Learning to Trust Each Other   93
12   The Trial Began   101

13   Discussing Consequences   109
14   For the Sake of the Relationship   119
15   Recognize the Tornadoes   130

Part 4
Becoming a Family

16   Becoming a Family Takes Time   141
17   Stepfathers and Sons   152
18   Stepfathers and Daughters   163
19   On Being a Stepmother   171
20   No Competition Please   180
21   The Ultimate Blending Glue   187

Acknowledgments

When I was a teenager my mother died of cancer, causing my dad to raise us as a single parent. After a time of struggling to raise his boys alone, my dad remarried and my stepmother, Lisa Barnes, entered our home. Only in recent years have I realized how difficult an adjustment it must have been for her to help raise two boys. Prior to marrying my dad, she never had any experience raising boys.

I have had the privilege of working in a residential program since 1974. This program, Sheridan House, offers residential care for teenagers with behavioral problems. Work with the families associated with this program has spawned my first three parenting books. Only as I was halfway through this particular book was I reminded of the fact that I too grew up in this same situation. One night, while writing, it occurred to me, *Hey, I grew up in a stepparent home too.*

There are many true stories and anecdotes in this book. The names and details have been changed to preserve the privacy of the people involved.

This book is dedicated as a thank-you for my stepmother's efforts to raise two boys who were difficult to love. It is written with the hope that other stepparents will find encouragement as they read.

Introduction

Ten-year-old Danny stood rigid as a board with his lower lip protruding. Looking his stepfather square in the eye Danny said, "You can't tell me what to do! You're not my daddy!"

Bill had been told that this day would come. He had been warned during premarital counseling to be prepared for the time when Danny would verbally challenge Bill's right to be a father figure in the new home.

Bill and Diane had only been married for two months. Prior to that time they dated for more than a year. It was a second marriage for both of them. While they were dating they made every attempt to help little Danny feel comfortable with their growing relationship. Bill even went so far as to take this little ten-year-old out for breakfast a few times.

Danny seemed very happy to have a new man who was giving him a lot of attention. On one occasion little Danny even said, "I hope you become my new daddy." With that vote of confidence from Danny, Bill felt it would be an easy transition. The little boy didn't appear to have any problem accepting a new father figure into his home and life.

Prior to the marriage, however, the dating situation portrayed a very unrealistic environment. The man-child relationship was only one of giving attention. Bill supplied Danny with a large extra dose of fun activities. This put one more person in the little boy's life—an adult friend who was able to play with him and listen to his stories.

Generally speaking this whole premarital adult-child relationship is misleading to the child. The child sees a man coming into his life who is acting like a friend. The man is probably also even buying him little extra treats. Mom has not been able to spend as much time with her son as she would like to, so Danny is starved for this extra attention. Mom has also been unable to spend much money on her son because of her desperate financial situation. This new man even has the time and money to take Danny and his mom out to get a hamburger and this is very exciting for the child.

My own son once asked me, "Daddy, do you think there are any children living in the North Pole with Santa Claus?" My son, who was four years old at the time, only thought of Santa Claus as someone who gave away toys. With that picture in mind he imagined how wonderful it would be to live with Santa Claus all year round and receive toys every day. There was no way my little son could have possibly understood that the rest of the year would have meant work and discipline to get ready for Christmas.

Children and even their parents go into stepparent relationships with similar dreams. "After we're all one big family, life will consist of going out for hamburgers every day." Life during the courtship period can be very unrealistic—almost a fantasy world. Family life cannot be built on the fantasies and gifts of courtship. Families must be built on the foundation of love, understanding and personal discipline from everyone. Building this foundation takes time.

When little Danny blurted out the statement, "You're not my daddy," he was really saying, "Prove it." Danny wanted to know if that man really wanted to be his daddy during the hard times as well as the hamburger times. Therein lies the answer. It all takes time as well as a plan to make two families one. Then will come the moment when little Danny can know that he now has another daddy who loves him.

The intention of this book is to help that process happen. The blending of preestablished families is a difficult procedure. It doesn't just happen automatically at a marriage ceremony. Nor does it happen simply because a couple puts in the years. There are various bridges that must be crossed. I hope these pages will provide a helpful map.

Part 1

Before the Step-Parenting Begins

1 | Before the Marriage Takes Place

Is he going to become my new daddy?" five-year-old Billy asked his mom. The question was awkward at best. The timing of the question was even more disastrous. Billy was standing next to his mom at a picnic while she was busily engaged in conversation with the man who had brought her to the event. It was at this moment that Billy decided to blurt out his question.

Fortunately, Billy's mom, Sarah, was prepared for just such an embarrassing moment. He had asked the question before. In fact, every time Sarah had involved herself in any kind of relationship Billy took it upon himself to pop the question. Even if Sarah was only interested in a platonic, friendly relationship, Billy seemed eager to ask.

It seemed logical to this little boy to ask such questions. After all, he wanted to know what was going on. Sarah was able to deal calmly with the question by answering, "No, Honey, I'm just spending time with a friend."

This little boy's question showed the anticipation in his heart. It may have signaled many kinds of emotions. Some children like Billy are eagerly waiting for the opportunity to experience what they imagine it would be like to have a dad in the house. *Imagine* is the key word here.

In the past they may have had a terrible time watching their parents disagree or even worse. As time has gone on, however, they have begun to dream of what it would be like to have the ideal father figure in the home—someone who would take them places and be available to do things with them all the time. They wonder about a man to play catch with and help them build model airplanes. Many children begin to create their own father figure.

Other children in a single-parent home still have a relationship with the male parent even though they don't live with him. The thought of Mom's remarrying places them in a dilemma. It would be nice to have the attention of another adult but would this force them to betray their noncustodial natural father or mother? How would the parent with whom they don't live respond to a new marriage? Would that parent no longer take an interest in the child? Many questions like these may seem scary. The bottom line here is, Would my mom's new marriage cause me to lose my natural father? *If so*, the child may reason, *then my mission may be to sabotage any new marriage.*

One child could be anxious to have a father figure in the home. Another child might be worried about what a new father figure might do to his relationship with his natural father. Then there is a third scenario that many children may imagine. Some children have spent many years in a single-parent home and they have become very comfortable with the arrangement. The child or young person has all of Mom's attention and has no desire to share her with anyone else. The thought of Mom's spending her Friday evening on a date with someone other than her offspring is very threatening to the child. These are three different situations that could even be taking place with three children in the same home. It is important for a parent to find out what the child is thinking—which of these emotions the child is experiencing.

Since 1974 I have had the pleasure of working at Sheridan House Family Ministries. One of our services is residential treatment centers for teenage boys and girls. In other words, we operate several homes for children. Every few years we start the process rolling to build another new home. It's a massive endeavor and once the land has been donated our architect, Glen Pate, begins the project by walking around the new property.

Glen has taught me much about the process of beginning a new house. I used to think that you simply acquired some property, chose some house plans that you liked and then hired a builder. "Oh no," Glen once said to me. "As your architect it's my job to help you blend the house to the land." As we began the process of adjusting our house plans I realized how important it is to think through the process long before the actual building begins.

Funny thing about an architect. He looks at things very objectively. There are no "sacred cows." Glen had no emotional attachment to the plans or the property. It was his job to help fit the two together. Where he found things that hindered the blend of the house plans and the property he made changes. It was very valuable, though often painful, to have the help of that unemotional perspective. It's easier and less costly to make corrections before the building begins than it is to make changes after the building is up. After-the-fact remodeling is a major headache.

The same is obviously true for the marriage of two families. Before the marriage takes place, in fact, before dating takes place, is the time to make some decisions. Objective plans can be made before dating begins. Often once dating has started, objectivity flies out the window.

Decisions need to be made concerning the way the child will be involved or not be involved with any dating situations or events. Some children may be better off not interacting with various friends of the opposite gender. They get their hopes up and are only disappointed when it's just a casual dinner date.

Parents will also want to decide just how much they are going to permit their children to be dated or "romanced" by the would-be suitor. This will be discussed further in another chapter. Suffice it to say here that children cannot distinguish between a gift that is no more than a nice gesture and a commitment to a relationship. Some children so deeply need a relationship that they can easily read much more into gifts than is meant. "Does the gift mean that this man really likes me and wants to be my new dad?" The courtship situation has too many dynamics for a child to understand. After all, the adults involved aren't really sure of each other's intentions. How can one expect the child to be able to keep up with what is going on? Keep the child out of the courtship.

The little boy at the beginning of this chapter wanted to know if this man was going to be his new daddy. It was almost as if he were looking at a possible new piece of land to build a new house. He wanted to begin imagining what the house would be like if it were built there, or in this case he wanted to imagine what it would be like if this were to become his mom's new husband.

Make Rules Before You Make Mistakes

Before two families are blended there must be rules. These rules are for the sake of the child as well as the adults involved. There are three steps to help establish these rules of courtship. One way is for the single parent to think through and decide the ground rules for dating and engagement before any dating begins. This sounds much easier to do than it really is. It is much easier to establish rules when one is not dating. Then when the whirlwind of the much-awaited dating process begins, the rules often go out the window.

Get Accountable

The second step is to find a group for accountability. This used to be the role of the extended family. Often an extended family is not available in today's society, however. It is very important that single parents find some group to whom they can become accountable. This closeness means that they will be held accountable for their actions and decisions when the emotions of dating take over.

Because a single parent's mother and father may be back in Cincinnati when she finds herself living in Southern California, a very dangerous situation can develop. She is seemingly held accountable to no one because there is no family around. The new extended family in today's society is the church. The best move a single parent can make is to find a support system or Bible study group within the church. Such a group should love them enough to confront the real issues and discrepancies in the parent's courtship behavior.

Find a Third Party

The third step in the process of dating should take place after a couple has begun to talk about the possibility of marriage. The help of a marriage counselor or pastor should be sought. A counselor will help each party look objectively at the relationship and the hurdles that are present in the possible blending of the two families. It is important not to wait too long to seek premarriage counseling. Many couples wait until they are too emotionally committed to the marriage to see the magnitude of the hurdles due to their emotional high. Many couples have left a church because a loving pastor tried to warn them to wait a while longer. Feeling persecuted by the pastor, the couple left rather than listened. Some return later only to say they wished they had listened. Couples should seek relationship counseling early enough in the dating process to allow them to listen.

It is the pastor or counselor's job to be the architect. An "architect-counselor" can help the couple talk about the difficulties that must be overcome before the house can be built on the land. The architect is there to help smooth over the difficult terrain.

Building a new house means spending time analyzing the land first. Then make some decisions long before bringing the house and land together. This will help the child understand what is going on. Long before people become stepparents the children are forced to think through the possibility. There are so many emotions and thoughts the child must process. A wise single parent will allow the child opportunities to talk and help the child interpret his feelings. Is he wondering whether he is being displaced in his mother's heart? Are his expectations too great? Perhaps the most difficult concern to confront is the possible thought that he is betraying his natural father's love. There is so much to deal with and yet so little understanding.

The wise single parent will be extremely careful how he or she handles the dating process. At the same time the parent will keep the parent-child lines of communication and interpretation open.

Summary

1. Children in the single-parent home have one or more emotions to deal with when their parent is dating.

   a. *Excitement* because they have unrealistic expectations about all the things this new marriage is going to bring into their lives personally. They expect fun and activities all the time.

   b. *Fear* that if they accept this new person into their lives it will be seen as a betrayal of their natural, non-custodial father (or mother). Will their father be angry at them or not want to see them any more?

   c. *Panic* that this new husband is replacing the child in their mother's heart. *When Mom marries him I won't be her best friend and main companion anymore.*

2. Dating/Engagement ground rules:

   a. *Rules* for dating must be set before the dating process and all its emotions begin.

   b. A *support group* should be in place before dating starts. Without one the single parent is too vulnerable.

   c. A *counselor* should be sought as the dating situation begins to get serious.

3. The parent must strive to keep the lines of communication open with the child. Many times that will mean

helping the child interpret what his or her true feelings are when it comes to seeing Mom date.*

*Quite often in this book the parent will be referred to in the female gender. I am well aware that many of the single parents who are in the blending process are also fathers. In fact, due to the death of my mother, I was raised by a single father and went through the blending process when a step*mother* rather than a step*father* came into our home. For the sake of the flow of the writing, however, the custodial parent will generally be referred to as a mom. It would become too cumbersome to continually say "mother or father." "Mother" and "stepfather" will be used when referring to all blended family configurations. I will also often use the generic "he" and "him" when referring to the child, even though girls are as affected by divorce as are boys.

2 | The Guilt of the Child

Connie sat in my office and talked about her parents' divorce. It quickly became apparent that I was hearing a very familiar story. This twelve-year-old was experiencing some guilt over the separation and divorce of her parents.

"Connie, do you feel that you played a part in your parents' divorce?" I asked.

"What do you mean?" she responded defensively.

"Well, as far as you know, what do you think were the things that caused your parents to get divorced?" I asked again. This time she unloaded a misguided perception that she had carried on her heart for a long time.

"I guess my parents got divorced because they couldn't get along with each other. My mom says there was a lot of stress on the two of them back then and they just couldn't take it any more so they got divorced."

It was a very rote answer, as if she had used it several times but didn't really believe it. Probing deeper I asked her, "You sound as if you don't really believe that. What do you think happened?"

Connie sat quietly for a moment as if she were hoping I would pick up the conversation. After a moment she said, "I think that I was born at the wrong time for them, and I caused a lot of problems for them. If I hadn't been born when I was, I think they would still be together. I should have just acted better when I was little."

Many family counselors have heard the same story over and over—a child who has grown up believing that she was the cause of her parents' divorce. Perhaps it was something the child did or the way the child behaved. Connie had convinced herself that it couldn't have been her parents who caused the divorce. After all, both of her parents were wonderful people, regardless of what anybody else said. The divorce must have been caused by the child.

Research indicates that Connie's case is typical. Jellinek and Slovik report in the *New England Journal of Medicine* (September 3, 1981) that children who go through divorce at a young age are especially vulnerable to these feelings of guilt. Young children cannot understand the complex problems that lead to a divorce. Though the marital problems may have been blatantly obvious and easy for any adult to see, this is not necessarily true for the young child. Young children go through a stage of developing their own personal conscience and feeling of responsibility. This new growth in the area of personal accountability can touch off feelings of guilt when the child hears the parents arguing about everything including the child himself. He can easily lead himself to feel guilt. From there the child fantasizes that he is the real cause of the divorce. This particular study sums it up well with a quote from a preschool child of divorce. "I am a bad boy . . . if only I hadn't . . . then Daddy would be home."

In Connie's case, she was only two years old when her parents separated. The fact that no one had really been able to give her a good reason for the divorce led her to believe it must have been her fault. She asked often enough, but the only thing either parent ever said was, "Oh, I don't know, Honey. We just couldn't get along together any more."

Other times children hear explanations like, "We got to the point that all we ever did was argue." Some children have made themselves believe that the arguments must have been about them. "As a baby I cried a lot, so they had to be up all night with me," a boy once told me. "If only I had been an easier baby I think my parents would still be together."

More bizarre than that is the story of the young boy who used to dream of what life would be like without his mom. He loved his mom very much but his dad was a businessman who worked long hours. His mother held down the home front while Dad worked. He used to imagine that if Mom had to go away for a while, his dad would have to be home more. Then without any warning it happened. One night his mother died of cancer. For years that little boy went to bed imagining that since he had thought about such a horrible thing he had actually caused or willed his mother's death. He couldn't talk to his dad about it because the boy didn't want his dad to think he had done something horrible. The guilt that child carried around with him was enormous.

Sound like a preposterous story? Oh, it's not. I know that story well because I was that boy. It's astounding the things that some children have concocted in their minds to explain the divorce or loss of a parent. Ridiculous or not, it's a thought that remained in the back of my mind throughout the latter part of my teenage years.

Children take the few facts that they have and work with them as best they can. Their desire is to find an explanation for the divorce. When they ask the logical questions, it's often very difficult, if not damaging, to give the correct answers. Due to their age at the time of the separation it is often impossible or unwise to fully explain to them the real causes of the divorce. It might destroy their image of one parent—or the reasons wouldn't make sense anyway. The children are then left to fill in the blanks. Many times they put their names in those blanks.

This guilt must be dealt with before the child and parent can attempt to go on with life. It will be very difficult for a custodial parent to attempt another marriage without helping the child deal with the causes for the end of the previous one. It will be impossible for the child to develop a relationship with a new adult in his life without first dealing with any misguided feelings he might have about the divorce of his parents.

Create an Open Atmosphere

There are steps that should be taken by single parents to help the child air and deal with any guilt he might be feeling about the divorce. The first step is to create an atmosphere that would allow the child to talk about any misperception he might have about the divorce. Many single parents are shocked to find out that their children carry with them such feelings of guilt.

"That's absolutely ridiculous," Connie's mother said to me. "How could she possibly feel that way? She was a little baby. We got divorced because her father couldn't stay out of bed with other women. What am I supposed to do—tell this little girl that her father is a womanizer?"

This mother exploded with rage as well as her own guilt. Rage that the divorce and her former husband's problems were still hurting the family. Guilt that she had been unable to answer her daughter's questions in a satisfactory way. Her question, fired at me, was very real. What was she to tell her child?

Some Reassuring Answers Must Be Given

To avoid telling Connie the awful truth about her father, the mother had chosen to tell her daughter nothing. She was right not to share the ugly details. But she was wrong to leave her daughter to fill in her own blanks. Children must be relieved of as much pain as possible. That means there have to be some answers given.

"None of this makes sense to me," Connie's mom went on to say. "If Connie has these guilt feelings, and if this is the cause for some of her behavior, then why hasn't she come to me to talk about it?"

Connie's mom might have said, "You know, Connie, sometimes I feel as if you think that you played a part in causing the divorce. Nothing could be further from the truth. Your father and I just could not stay married. He decided that he wanted to be with another woman and I had to let him go. The only thing that kept him here for so long was his love for you. I want to say that again. You were good for our marriage, not bad for it. If you feel that you are partly to blame for our divorce, you couldn't be more wrong."

It's asking a lot to expect children to express the real questions in their hearts. Even adults find it difficult to come right out and bluntly ask the difficult questions of life: "Excuse me, Mom, did I cause you and Dad to get divorced?" Worse yet, the child would really be asking, "Am I the one who caused us to go through all this misery? I mean, is it my fault that you are in your bedroom crying most nights?"

Impossible! There is just no way a child could ask those questions, but parents must still attempt to answer these unstated misconceptions. Parents must learn to read between the questions or listen to the silence. Why are the children asking so many questions? Or maybe the opposite is true. Why do they avoid all talk about the divorce when this is something that has had such a tremendous impact on their lives? Maybe they are afraid that answers will only confirm what they have come to believe. Parents must create an open-door policy. All questions are acceptable, no matter how many times they are asked. Let the children talk about it. When they don't talk, parents must find a way to open these doors.

There are times when children and young people are more open for discussion. Usually these are times when parents find themselves the busiest. Bedtime is one of those times for many children. In the darkness of a bedroom many children are able to ask the questions troubling them. Parents would do well to lie down beside the child and listen to the questions behind the questions. There is something about a dark room where both parent and child are facing the ceiling. I think it also helps that the child knows his parent can't see his face when he is asking difficult questions.

Listen at Bedtime

Take advantage of bedtime. Parents should arrange their schedule so as to be able to spend fifteen minutes on the bed with the child. Small children will usually be more than happy to discuss anything at this hour—anything to delay going to sleep. Take advantage of this.

In addition to allowing discussion, parents must listen. Listening takes time—something that is in tight supply for most single parents. Time and concentration will be necessary, however, in order to hear what a child's heart is saying.

"Billy never talks about the divorce," Melinda told me. "Jack and I were divorced when Billy was three and now he's eight and doesn't want to talk about it. In fact, when I bring it up he actually says things that let me know he doesn't want to talk about it."

That, in itself, is a statement. Billy's refusal may be saying that he has some very bad feelings about the divorce or that he just doesn't want some of his thoughts verified through discussion. That's no reason to avoid the discussion. Everyone may feel more comfortable avoiding the discussion, but that feeling of comfort is only temporary. This mom needed to answer the question that her son's silence was really asking.

"You know, Billy, every time I bring up your father's and my divorce you roll over in bed. Ah, see there you go again. It's okay to roll over and face the wall, but tonight I'm going to keep talking. Tonight I'm going to have your bear ask me some questions that I think he needs to hear the answers to."

That mom should not even say, at this point, "Is that okay?" The child doesn't know whether it's okay or not because he doesn't know whether he's going to want to hear the answer. However, he still needs some answers that can settle some unasked questions.

Bear (Mom changing her voice to Bear's voice): Billy might not want to know but I want to know—why did you and Daddy get divorced?

Mom: Daddy and I got divorced because there were some very serious problems in our marriage. We got to the point that we didn't love each other any more and

Daddy decided that he loved another lady more than me.

Bear: Why? Why did Daddy love another lady more than you?

Mom: I don't know the answer to that question, but he did. Some of it might have been my fault. I do know one thing, however, and it's very important that you tell this to Billy. Daddy and I stayed together much longer than we would have because of Billy. We both love Billy very much and Billy was the best thing about our marriage. The fact that Billy was such a blessing to our marriage kept our marriage together for a long time. Daddy just didn't want to leave you (I mean Billy). Bear, will you be sure that Billy understands what I've just said?

At this point one mother, using a doll for this discussion, said that her daughter took over the doll's voice and asked a question. It was a very crucial point to the reality of this bedtime discussion. The doll asked, "If Daddy loves his little girl so much, then why don't we see him any more? Why doesn't he come to take her out like he used to?"

Every situation is different. In many divorced homes today the noncustodial parent or the shared custodial parent spends as much time as possible with the children. This is not true in all cases, however. In homes such as these this often unasked question must be addressed.

Many times the biggest proof the child has that he or she caused the divorce is just this fact. "If Daddy did love me, he would want to see me. The fact that he doesn't see me must mean he doesn't want to." To give a totally comforting answer to this particular concern is impossible. But the child cannot be allowed to use his father's absence as the basis for his misperception that he caused the divorce. It must be dealt with. Mom needs to go back into Bear's voice.

Bear: If Daddy does love us so much, how come we don't

get to see him any more? Why does he spend time with that other lady's kids and not us?

Mom: I don't know why Daddy doesn't come to see us. I do know that he loves Billy very much. I also know that Billy didn't cause the divorce. In fact, it was Mom and Daddy's great love for Billy that kept them together for so long. Billy helped our marriage. Please tell that to Billy. Maybe Daddy feels bad about leaving Billy so he doesn't come to see him. I don't know. All I do know is that Billy was the best thing that happened in our marriage. Do you have any other questions Bear?

(a moment of silence)

This talk was very helpful to me, Bear. I would like to do it again tomorrow night. Is that okay, Bear?

This kind of dialogue, where Mom talks in her own voice, as well as the voice of the child's stuffed animal, will often help open doors for a young child. Older children may need the stuffed animal removed from the dialogue. The important thing is that the discussion is open and that the questions needing to be dealt with are talked about. The child or young person needs to be relieved of his guilt. If not, it will cause damage in future relationships.

Guilt is something that often takes root, growing into bitterness and anger. All these emotions are debilitating. They must be dealt with emotionally as well as spiritually. Parents would do well to help their children understand that there are some things in life we should feel guilty about—such as lies that we tell or mean things that we may say to others. The way to deal with those kinds of guilt is to ask the offended party to forgive us and to ask God for forgiveness.

On the other hand, there are feelings of guilt that are wrong. In an attempt to search for explanations, people often blame themselves and feel guilty. That guilt will eventually fester into anger. It must be talked about and dealt with. This serves as advice for the parent as well as the child.

"But my fourteen-year-old daughter refuses to talk about it. No matter what I try she won't talk and I know she's really hurting. I think she feels it will only hurt me if we really talk."

In situations where an older child refuses to talk and all avenues for dialogue have been tried, it's time to seek outside help. It's important to get a child to counseling, no matter what the cost. When inappropriate feelings are not dealt with properly the child or young person could be handicapped in future relationships. Get help when your child won't or is unable to talk about concerns that you can sense must be addressed. Guilt, especially misguided guilt, can crush a person's heart.

Summary

1. Many children believe that they played a part in bringing about the divorce. This can cause the child to feel tremendous guilt. *What kind of a child am I? I caused my parents to get divorced!*

2. Guilt often results because parents are unable to give the child a reason for the divorce. Parents often refuse to talk about it.

3. The child must be allowed to talk about the divorce.

4. The parents must give the best answers they can as to the reasons for the divorce, without giving details.

5. The child must be relieved of the feeling that he caused the divorce.

6. Even if the child doesn't actually ask the questions, the parent must find a creative way to answer the questions. The parent must open up the lines of communication about this very important topic.

7. When a young person is unable to discuss the divorce and yet the parent knows that he is hurting, outside

help should be sought.

8. Guilt left to fester can make future relationships very difficult.

3 | Romancing the Child

Have you ever done something or committed to something only to find out later that it was very different than you expected? Many newlywed wives are shocked at the difference between the man they dated and that same person after they are married. Prior to the wedding he was exciting and fun to be around. There were romantic dinners and big events to impress her. He was even nice to her parents. It was all part of the dating game. Putting his best foot forward, it was only natural for the suitor to attempt to make everyone concerned think he was wonderful.

After the wedding, the courting stopped. Unfortunately, so did the suitor's attempts to meet everyone's needs. No matter what the setting is, the "game" is played when a boy tries to win his girlfriend's hand. Or a corporation is trying to lure an executive to join the company. It could even be a church trying to entice a potential pastor by putting its best foot forward. It's human nature to try to get what you want by attempting to impress everyone involved in the decision-making process.

Adults are supposed to be mature enough to deal with these allurements. They are supposed to be able to distinguish reality from fiction. Adults may be able to do that but children cannot. Children should not be permitted to be a part of the romancing process when two families are blending.

The Natural Salesman

Frank was a natural salesman. He didn't know that he shouldn't try to win the hand of the children as well as their mother. Barbara was a divorced mother of two. Frank was very interested in a deeper relationship with Barbara. They had dated for quite some time, but Barbara had put the brakes on the relationship. She had too much responsibility raising her two boys to get into a serious relationship.

Everyone knows that one of the best ways to help a relationship grow is to find a common interest. Any good salesman knows that if he has a potential client who seems to be slipping through his fingers, he better find out how to get closer to that person. If the client loves golf, the salesman takes him for a round of golf. If fishing is his client's interest, they go fishing.

Barbara's basic interest in life was her two boys. Frank decided that he would show an interest in Barbara's sons. It is said that the way to get to a man's heart is through his stomach. That may or may not be true. It is certain, however, that the way to get to a woman's heart is to pay attention to her children.

Toys for the Boys

Frank not only showed an interest in the boys, he went much further. He began to buy toys and other surprises for them. Frank got close enough to the family to talk with the boys, listen to them, and learn about the things they liked. The boys quickly learned that if they mentioned a toy that wasn't too expensive, it would soon be theirs. The next time "Uncle Frank" appeared he would have it wrapped as a little surprise for them.

This became a mutual, unspoken arrangement between man and boys. The boys enjoyed being with Frank because of his gifts and the exciting events to which he took them. Frank appeared to be a model male figure for the boys.

This relationship looked like everything Barbara could ask for in a father and husband—in just that order. She wasn't really in love with Frank, but he was so good to the boys. All they ever talked about was "Uncle Frank this" and "Uncle Frank that." Her real feeling for Frank could be better stated as, perhaps she *should* learn to love him.

The whole relationship was built on deception. Frank deceived Barbara and the boys by romancing the children as well as the mom. Children are easy marks and it's unfair to play upon their desires. Frank was doing things and purchasing presents for these children that Barbara could not afford. The children and Barbara fell for the whole package, Frank and all.

The children, however, were also accomplices in this deception. It wasn't really Uncle Frank whom they loved to be with. It was the excitement and gifts that came in the door with him. In fact, they really didn't know Uncle Frank at all.

The Root of the Problem

This masquerade set everyone up for tremendous disappointment. As bad as it was that the children and Frank were playing this symbiotic game, it was Barbara who was the most to blame. Barbara's job as a parent should have been to protect her children from entanglements with would-be suitors. She should not have allowed her boys to be involved in a dating triangle. Children are just too vulnerable. Just as the courtship ends in the male-female relationship shortly after the marriage takes place, the courtship with the children vanishes.

It is not unusual for stepparents to attempt to buy the affections of the children. The stepparent adopts the role of rescuer. The child is lacking for many things. As the stepparent tries to blend the family, it becomes easier to buy the family. When the buying stops the family is thrown into turmoil.

"I don't know what these kids want," Frank, now a stepfather, said in the counseling room. "Barbara and I got married and it was fun to buy for them. Then they started acting snooty toward me when I came home without a gift. They would run to the door to meet me, but as soon as they saw I was not carrying any presents they'd walk away from me disgusted. What kind of greedy little kids are they? They act like it's my job to bring them something every day."

That was exactly right. The children expected a gift a day because that was what they were taught to expect. When everyone was on their best behavior the gifts would flow freely. As soon as the children started to act more like normal children, and misbehaved, the gifts stopped.

Gifts and Games

If you build a relationship around the giving of things, the children will expect you to give gifts. As long as that continues, the stepparent and child will never get to know each other. They will continue to play games to get the prizes. There will never be a blending of the family where the members learn to love and respect each other; they will only learn to get things from each other.

The mother (or natural parent) of the children must not allow the children to be romanced during the courting stages. Nor should she allow her new husband to shower the children with presents at the beginning stages of the marriage. It will only give the children unrealistic expectations.

"Honey, I appreciate the way you want to do so many things for the kids. I really think that we need to slow down, though. They're not used to all this overindulgence. It's much better for us to spend time as a family, playing games and learning more about each other."

Many times buying big gifts and staying involved constantly in big activities are only an avoidance. It only causes stepparent and child to avoid getting to know each other and retards the relationship process. A stepparent may mean well by acting like Santa Claus, but it will only confuse the child. Mom needs to help the two factions (stepparent and child) take the time to *blend* rather than *spend*.

One of the most difficult things for stepparent and child to do is to blend. It takes experiences where the two of them are simply spending time together, and that is often intimidating for the adult. "I don't know what to do with this child," a man said. "I realize now that it was just easier for me to *do* for the child rather than just *be* with him. If I buy something I won't have to think of what to say or do together. I see that my insecurities about this relationship have only postponed our blend as a family."

Summary

1. It may be natural for a suitor to romance the children while dating the mom, but this will prove to be a damaging approach to the relationship.

2. New stepparents should not attempt to act like rescuers by taking on the role of gift-givers.

3. The natural parent holds the strings in these symbiotic relationships. She should not permit the children to be "bought" by a suitor or new stepparent. This romancing of the children will only cause confusion. It is the job of the natural parent to keep the children out of the dating process. It is also the job of the parent to advise a new stepparent about the danger of attempting to purchase a child's love.

Part 2

What's Happening to This New Family?

4 | Am I Crazy or Is This Child Actually Trying to Sabotage Our Marriage?

In exasperation a stepfather sat in front of me and tried to explain the strange process that was taking place in his new home. "It seems as if we have been on a roller coaster since our marriage. In fact, I sometimes find myself actually afraid to say to Donna [his wife] that things are going better. Just as soon as we have a good time as a family, we take a major nosedive."

This stepfather went on to describe how his family would do things together and have a wonderful time. They might go to the park one day and actually act like a family that was in love with each other. That night this dad would lie in bed and say to his wife, "Today was great, wasn't it? I think the kids are starting to accept me and my place in the home."

No sooner would he make this comment than everything would cave in the next morning. The kids would be fighting, and they would question his authority to intervene. Worse than that, they might want to talk to their mother in private about their natural father and the fact that they don't like this new arrangement. The up-and-down cycle led this stepfather finally to blurt out his frustration, "This may sound ridiculous to you, and I don't really want to sound paranoid, but I've reached the point where I wonder if these children are actually trying to sabotage our marriage."

This doesn't sound ridiculous at all. As a matter of fact, in a perverse way it might make sense to the children. They might have caught themselves having too much fun as a family. Perhaps they were actually enjoying themselves with this new parent. When this happens they might have felt an obligation to interfere with all this harmony.

In Chapter 1, I discussed the child's feelings of guilt over the divorce. The guilt children carry around is not the end of the story. Children often dream of negative ways of dealing with that guilt. What better way for a child to imagine himself dealing with the guilt than to redeem himself in the eyes of his family? Feeling somehow accountable for the divorce, the child often searches for ways of putting everything back together. "If I could help my parents get back together, then everything would be wonderful," twelve-year-old Connie finally blurted out that day in my office. This thought process is more common in small children, but it has been my experience that children and young people of all ages carry this dream to some extent.

The Dream Stage is often the next step after the Guilt Stage. This second stage doesn't actually replace the first one, but it fuels it. There are two very typical dreams that often take place and become the driving force in the child's behavior.

Dream Number One

The first dream many children carry, above all others, is that their parents will get back together. When their parents get back together, everything will be great. Notice the use of the word *when*. This very powerful dream often consumes a child's thoughts. It's not a matter of "if" the parents get back together, but rather "when" they do. When the family is back together, the child dreams, everything will be different. Everyone in the family will try harder, and everyone will finally be just like he dreamed a picture-perfect family should be.

It doesn't matter to children that this might be an impossible dream. They don't seem to remember how horrible it was when Mom and Dad were together. They forget the fact that there was constant bickering, physical abuse, or drunkenness. Given another chance, it will all be different.

The fact that both parents have moved on with their lives can also be irrelevant. The child's parents may have even gone on to marry other people. Just as his feelings of guilt were totally misguided, so too are his dreams of reconciliation. Regardless of the situation many children still carry the dream.

The Second Dream:
The Humpty-Dumpty Fantasy

The second dream takes the first dream one step further. The child dreams of the opportunity to redeem his guilt. A child who feels like he is the villain who played a part in causing the separation or divorce could now be a hero. If he worked hard he could be the one who puts the family back together again. Just like all the king's men in the Humpty-Dumpty nursery rhyme, he would like to be the one to put the family back together again.

Whether the child actually takes steps to manipulate the reconciliation or not varies from family to family. The reality of the dream, however, is very common. In the second dream, the child imagines himself as the great reconciler in this family tragedy.

Dreaming oneself to be a mediator is not so far-fetched. Some children dream they will become professional athletes or reach some other grandiose position in society. My son carried a dream of becoming a professional football player when he weighed only fifty-four pounds. Certainly it would seem somewhat more "realistic" and reachable for a child to dream of putting his family back together.

This little dream is sidetracked when the child's parent begins to show an interest in a new potential spouse. Connie's case was classic. The divorce had happened years before. After all those years of living alone, her mother remarried. Few of the tangible realities in this situation mattered to Connie. The fact that her father had remarried long ago mattered little to her. She still carried the dream. If there had been a divorce once, why not again?

The fact that her mother had not yet married was this girl's final hope. It was her mother she lived with day in and day out. The mother's new marriage was the final blow to the two dreams she had harbored for years. Not only did the prospect of reconciliation look impossible, but so did her dreams of being the heroic matchmaker.

Remaining consistent to her dreams, this little girl totally refused to accept her mother's new husband. His presence was the visible evidence that her dream was not coming true. Connie's answer was to act in such a way as to sabotage her mother's new marriage. Connie decided that if she was rotten enough maybe this new man would leave and then "my mom and dad could get back together again." She actually had reached the point where she derived some pleasure from seeing and hearing her mother and stepfather argue about her. It fit into her plan to redeem herself and be a heroine.

There are many children who might not even be aware that they are causing their new stepparent and parent to fight with each other. It just becomes a subconscious means to a conscious end. The child becomes very uncooperative, especially when the stepparent is in charge. He may do everything in his power to make it impossible for the stepparent to do anything to please him. No matter how hard the stepparent tries to be nice, or what this new parent attempts to do, it's wrong.

One teenager actually told me that it made her feel guilty to have fun with her new family. "I know it sounds silly," she said, "but after we play a game or go get ice cream, I sometimes feel guilty that I enjoyed it." She went on to say that the more fun she had with her new stepparent, the worse she felt afterwards. "I feel like I can't let myself go and laugh, or I will be doing something wrong." She would be betraying her dream. Almost as unthinkable, she felt as if she were being disloyal to her father.

A study by Wallerstein and Kelly (*The Child in His Family*, 1974) even indicated that some children consider floating from one parent's home to the other in an attempt to fulfill the dream. The child works hard at "keeping tabs" on each parent, trying to put the family and marriage back together. The study found that these efforts of floating back and forth, like a traveling ambassador of good will, might not end until one parent remarries.

The dream is there. As fictitious as it sounds, it may not be fiction to the child. Parents in blended families must attempt to understand the agony and the dream that the child might carry with him to bed each night. Once that is understood, a parent can take steps to deal with the problem.

Connie had never really given her stepfather a chance. She didn't know him for who he really was. Her only recent interaction with him had been her dealings with him as he responded to her "sabotage" efforts. Naturally her stepfather was both bewildered and angry that this child was acting in such an irrational way. He made efforts to unite the family and learn to love each family member; she, in turn, made efforts to be unlovable. He tried to pull the family together; Connie attempted to blow the new family apart. They were fighting a war that he didn't want to fight. What he didn't realize was that he wasn't really Connie's enemy. The child's dream was her enemy.

It's Not Really a Battle with the Stepparent

This is an extremely important point of awareness. "Why does she hate me so much?" a stepfather almost screamed. "I've never done anything but try to love her." It needs to be said again. The child caught in this dilemma doesn't hate the stepparent. She may hate the situation. Her dream is broken. It fell apart when the stepparent entered the scene. It is only natural for her to vent her frustration on the newest party on the block. Understanding that, the stepparent must work at a very difficult task. He cannot allow himself to take the child's behavior personally. Actually it is a protest of the divorce more than anything else. Granted, not taking the child's words and behavior personally is a tall order, but perhaps when it is understood it will be easier.

Keys to Survival

The keys to the survival of this stepparent home will be to decide to give it time. Love the child anyway. Work on the marriage and develop a parenting plan that both husband and wife agree upon, then give the child time. It takes nine months to birth a baby. During that time the parents have many weeks to think through their parenting strategies. They probably even got books to read to help them be better parents. Then as the baby grew they realized that they had to scrap some of their parenting ideas and develop new ones. The slow growth of the baby allowed them time to reevaluate. The same is true for the stepparent. Nothing will be accomplished overnight. Endurance is necessary. Actually, it's mandatory.

Children in this "new parent" situation often feel as though they have now lost everything. Their parents will never get back together and so all is over. Another key to helping them accept the new marriage is to show them that they have actually gained. It is not a gain of material things, but rather a gain in family happiness.

Families have personalities of their own. Some families are innately angry or constantly sad. Many single parents spend times when they are depressingly emotional. If you would ask a child what his family or home life is like perhaps he would say, "Lonely. It's lonely at our house and we never seem to do anything as a family anymore." The personality of that home would be one of sadness.

With a new marriage in the home that can change. Though there will be months of adjustment, there can also be fun. The new marriage should insert some adrenaline into the family. The child can eventually discover that he is actually laughing for the first time in months. With two adults in the home there should be more hands to get things done. That means more time for family activities.

It will take time, but eventually the child will realize that the family is gaining a healthier personality. They will actually be enjoying each other. Again it must be stressed: It will take time for the child to realize that the family stability seems to be strengthening. It's up to the parents. They can succumb to the doom and gloom of the children or they can fight it by arranging enriching family activities. The personality of the new stepparent home can make a major leap. This will help the child realize that this new marriage isn't as bad as he had dreamed it would be.

Several years ago a set of houseparents at Sheridan House for boys went to a three-day conference out of town. The duties of that particular home of ten teenage boys were temporarily left to another counselor and me. We moved into the house for three days. The boys were determined to make life miserable for us by acting bored the entire time.

Early one morning I was in the kitchen making scrambled eggs for breakfast. As I opened the cabinet next to the stove, in search of spices, I noticed an additional opportunity to "spice up" this glob of two dozen eggs—food coloring. I decided to dye the eggs blue. Unfortunately I didn't realize that blue die mixed with yellow eggs made the eggs a disgusting slime green.

One of the boys wandered into the kitchen and saw this massive glob of slime-green cooking on the skillet. "What is that!" he screamed in horror. Before I could say anything, my partner, Steve, said, "Iguana eggs. We're having a delicacy this morning. Scrambled Iguana eggs."

"Not me!" the boy yelled as he ran out of the kitchen. Before long all the boys were looking over my shoulder. They couldn't believe they would be served reptile eggs. Some believed the iguana story and some only acted as if they believed it. Regardless, they all complained as they were required to try one small spoonful of this "delicacy." The complaining was so incredible that I felt my attempt at fun was a dismal failure.

Later that morning I got a phone call from the dean at the school where these boys attend. "What in the world happened over there this morning?" the dean asked. When he said that, I knew it must have been a mistake to try to have this fun at breakfast.

"Why? What have they done?" I asked as my heart sank.

"Oh no! They haven't done anything wrong. In fact, they're actually getting along better than usual. I've never seen them walking to class laughing before. They're talking about iguana eggs all over school. Half the kids at Attucks Middle School want to come to Sheridan House for breakfast tomorrow."

I couldn't believe it. What I had perceived as a failure had actually drawn the boys together. They just didn't want to let me see them having fun or acting like a family.

Summary

1. Many children feel tremendous guilt about the separation or divorce of their parents. They actually have allowed themselves to believe that they caused the divorce.

2. Children of divorce often dream about their parents getting back together.

3. Some children do more than dream about the marriage getting back together. They also dream that they can redeem themselves by helping their parents get back together. That would not only get the family back together but it would make them the hero.

4. For that reason many children consciously or subconsciously sabotage their single parent's dating or their parent's new marriage. Their sole desire is to see their parents get back together no matter how impossible a situation that may be.

5. Parents can help by showing the child that the family is fun with the new stepparent in the home. The child can learn that it is not as bad as he expected. This can be accomplished with fun family activities or game nights.

5 | The Child Lost More Than He Gained

Debbie had a habit that is quite common among single moms. She let her little boy, Ben, spend many nights in her bed. In fact, Ben spent almost every night sleeping in Mommy's big bed.

Shortly after the divorce Ben would cry himself to sleep at night or complain of having nightmares. To calm him down, Debbie brought him into bed with her. It then became a nightly occurrence. Ben would manipulate a way to sleep with Mommy.

If she were to be honest with herself, Debbie would admit that she actually liked having her little boy with her. She didn't like his sticky little body adhered to her back all night. That only caused her to lose her much needed sleep. However, she did like waking up and seeing his little face. Ben was the beautiful by-product of an otherwise heart-breaking marriage. By sleeping in the same big bed both mother and child were doing each other a favor.

She had tried, without success, to get him back into his bed. *What harm could it do?* Debbie would ask herself. Now, sometime later, she was only too aware of the harm that it did. Debbie remarried after several years as a single parent. One of the most difficult things to do was to tell Ben that he could no longer sleep in the big bed with her. Worse than that, the bedroom door would be closed some nights. This was a crushing blow to her son.

Many single parents build an incredible intimacy with their children. This is important, as it helps the child know that the family is going to make it, even though one parent is no longer present. There must be a line of privacy, however. Children must be helped to learn that Mom needs some personal space or privacy. Without this lesson the child will resent any new intruder.

One family, coming for counseling, was having trouble with their oldest daughter. Mom was totally bewildered. "I don't understand what has happened to Laurie," the mom said. "She has been my most mature child. Not just because she's the oldest but because she was the most helpful. Now she is fighting us every step of the way."

Laurie had been her mother's special helper after the divorce. This twelve-year-old had taken it upon herself to grow up very quickly and accept many of the parental chores and responsibilities concerning the younger children. In so doing, she earned a special place in her mother's heart. In fact, Laurie spent many nights sitting up in Mom's room talking about the family. On some occasions her mother shared some very intimate things about the painful marriage and divorce. Through these times of communication Laurie became her mother's best friend.

The new marriage changed all that. Laurie was no longer her mother's most intimate companion. The ceremony transformed Laurie's role from adult back to child. This caused Laurie to have a great feeling of loss of position or status with her mother. One afternoon in counseling Laurie summed up her feelings well: "Parents always worry about who will lose custody of the children, but what about the children? Mom and Dad are remarried now and I feel like I have lost custody of my parents. For the first time I'm on the outside looking into both of their new lives."

No longer could Laurie sit up on Mom's bed and talk late into the night. No longer would Laurie share in the intimate stories her mother had to tell. Laurie's mom had a new best friend now and the loss was just too much to take. This teenager was angry.

Intimacy between parent and child is important. It would be very damaging to close a child out when the child already feels abandoned by the absent parent. The child needs an intimate relationship with the custodial parent. That line of privacy still must be drawn, however. The parent should resist going over the line of elevating the child to the point of being an adult. Many things the parent might feel a need to share with someone, should not be shared with a child. Children are not able to handle adult conversation or burdens.

Intimacy Must Be Lopsided

Parent-child intimacy needs to be one-way. The motive should be to meet the needs of the child rather than the needs of the parent. Some parents feel as if they are sharing details of the divorce because the child asked for them or to vindicate themselves. Chances are these are details that only an adult can process. Sharing them with a child should be resisted no matter how tempting it is.

Allowing the children to be children is important to the well-being and stability of the family. It will help the children to know that there is still an adult in charge of the family. If they are elevated to the status of adult by being taken into the confidence of the parent it could only cause them to become insecure about their family. "Who's really in charge here? Can my mom handle all the responsibility of being our parent?" This problem usually takes place with the oldest child—especially if that child is a daughter.

In many homes it seems only natural for a single mother to take her oldest daughter into her confidence. In her desperation for a friend to talk to about her crumbling life, the mom begins to talk with her daughter as if the girl were an adult. This robs the girl of her childhood and will only cause problems later on. Once this kind of intimacy is given, it is hard to retract it after a new marriage.

Personal Space Must Be Established

The second area to watch out for is personal space. Children need to be touched and hugged regularly. They also need to see that they will be okay away from Mom. One mom told me she couldn't even go to the bathroom with the door closed. Her son wanted to know that he had access to her at all times.

"I can't understand what the problem is," she pondered. "He spends all day away from me in day care and seems to do fine. When we get home it's a different story. I can't get two feet away from him."

We develop habits with our children. It's their job to push for as much of us as they can get. It's the parent's job to find a way to spend special time with the young child. Then the parent must also show the children that she needs her own time. Children may fight it, but it's healthy for the child to learn that Mom is not his own personal toy.

A monkey wrench gets thrown into the situation when the emotion of parental guilt comes into play. "After all, my child has had to go through so much already. I just can't help myself. When he asks if he can be with me all the time I just can't turn him away." This parent isn't responding out of a desire to meet the child's needs, she's responding to guilt. In reality the child needs to learn that Mom is there but that he can play by himself or sleep by himself and everything will be okay. By giving in to the child's push for her constant, undivided attention, the mom is hurting the child's development. She is also hurting the child's possibilities of accepting her future marriage.

This has even become evident in homes where the child's parents have come back together and remarried. Though the child thought that all he wanted was for his parents to get back together, he hadn't thought about the fact that it would mean he would lose some of Mom's attention. The mother fed Junior's desire to own Mom by pulling the child into bed with her at night and spending every at-home hour with the child. Now Dad's return to the home was only an interference in the child's unnaturally close relationship with his mom.

Parents must be careful to find a healthy balance. Yes, the child needs an intimate relationship with his parent. But it cannot be at the expense of pulling the child out of childhood. Little

Johnny or Debbie must not be made to fulfill the parent's need for a friend. Put the child in his own bed. Use the child's bedroom or the living room as a place for those special talks, not the parent's room. Try to maintain the master bedroom as a place of sanctuary and private space as much as possible. It will only make life easier for the child, should his father come home or a new marriage take place.

Now That We Are Already Married

"It's too late. Everything you are saying is all well and good, but now we are dealing with this very unhappy teenager. I've made all the mistakes you've mentioned. Where do we go from here?"

Laurie's parents were now at the place where they had to deal with their mistakes. There isn't a parent alive who doesn't have to spend time correcting parental mistakes. The key is for the parent to analyze the problem, think of a solution, and then implement it. There's just one more key to these problems: Give the child time to respond to the solutions.

Laurie was exhibiting a behavior that was new for her. Called rebellion, it didn't appear even when her mom was dating. That was because this mom would keep Laurie appraised of the dating situation. In fact, this mom would come home from a date and Laurie would be sitting up ready for a discussion of the evening. Laurie was still her mom's best friend. After the wedding, however, this new stepfather became Laurie's replacement. That's when Laurie felt the loss.

Laurie's two biggest hurts were the removal of responsibility and the loss of a friend. It happened overnight. In her excitement about this new marriage, her mom cut Laurie off completely. This can be partially avoided if the mother will continue to allow Laurie to carry out some of the family responsibilities. Laurie's primary need was to know that she still had her mother's love— that her mother still needed her. That need could be met only by Laurie's mother.

This mother needed to fight the urge to spend every waking moment with her new husband. As important as this might seem to the parent, it will only cause more problems with the children. It's only natural for this woman to think that she made many mistakes in her previous marriage and so she doesn't want to repeat them with this new husband. "Given another chance I know I will do a better job of focusing on the marriage." That's well said but the children will never understand it. All they know is that once they had Mom and now a man has come into her life and stolen her. There must be a balance. Yes, the marriage relationship is a priority, but not at the expense of totally ignoring the child.

Once Laurie's mom saw the picture for what it was, she realized that Laurie felt that she was no longer valuable to her mother. This concerned mom began to formulate a plan to help Laurie feel loved rather than replaced. For her family actually to blend, it was a mandatory priority.

Mrs. Smith, Laurie's mom, decided to set aside one breakfast a week for mother and daughter to go out. This was a time to talk and share their lives with each other. This was to replace those late nights they had spent together. Mrs. Smith did more than talk about the family or Laurie's life at school, though these areas were important. During each outing, she tried to find some little way to talk about her new marriage.

Mrs. Smith knew that it was important for Laurie to be able to discuss the topic of the marriage, which had previously been taboo. Laurie needed to feel free to talk and ask questions, however. There were other reasons that this wise mother brought up the marriage. Laurie might one day be married herself. All this young girl had known were the heartaches of marriage as she watched her mother go through the pain of divorce. Worse than that, Mrs. Smith had often told her about those heartaches. This mom wanted to undo those fears she had placed in her daughter's heart.

The only way for this mother and daughter to become intimate again was for them to be able to share the things that were most significant in their lives. The new marriage was certainly one of those items. So these prescheduled mother-daughter outings were to reopen the lines of communication, help the daughter feel valuable again, help the daughter feel more accepting of her new stepfather, and take advantage of an opportunity to teach the daughter about marriage.

The mother needs to be extremely wise and selective about what she discusses with her daughter. It needs to be a balance. There should be intimacy and yet the mother needs to realize that she is talking with a person who is not yet an adult, not able to handle adult topics. These discussions will be intimate if the mother discusses topics about the home where the daughter can feel that she has some input or advice. They can also discuss topics that will be instructive for the daughter. This could include discussions about the new marriage so the daughter can hear about a healthy relationship without violating some of the intimacies about the marriage. She must be careful never to share anything negative that might subvert the stepfather's role in the home.

Certainly this took time. That's why Mrs. Smith had to put these occasions into her calendar. At the same time her new husband had to be understanding as he made breakfast for the other children. It was time well spent, however, as Laurie grew to feel valuable and loved again.

One other time frame can be used for great impact, and that's bedtime. Parents can take advantage of the opportunity for communication at bedtime. Instead of bringing the child into the big bed, parents can lie down in the child's bed for fifteen minutes or more and allow the child the time for talk. It's important for the parent not to dominate the conversation. Allow the child the time to talk about whatever he wants. Allow the child the opportunity of having Mom all to himself a little bit each night.

All of this takes planning and time. Without spending time together, the child will only wither at the loss of a parent. Many parents are so ecstatic at the joy of their new marriage that they escape into the new relationship. That escape will not last long. The pain of the children will break through the bubble and cause the parents to take notice of the needs around them. It is better to start with a plan that gives the children some special parent-child time of their own. It is better to allow the oldest or only child an opportunity to feel as if his opinion is still valued. Break down the barriers of loss so that the children can begin to accept their new stepparent. Often they are not really rejecting the new stepparent, but rather the new situation that has caused them to lose their friend.

Summary

1. Children in single-parent homes must not be allowed to totally consume their parent's life.

2. Parents (especially single parents) need their own personal space. Get the child out of your bed.

3. Often, when a parent remarries, children feel that they have lost their parent or best friend.

4. The oldest child often feels pushed out of an intimate relationship with the parent. The oldest child may feel replaced by the stepparent or even replaced by the return of the estranged natural parent. That feeling will not help the family blend or get back together.

5. Quite often the stepparent is not the source of the child's anger. Even though he may be venting his anger or displeasure at the stepparent, it may actually be the new living situation that makes him angry.

6. The parent must make plans to spend private time with the children to help them feel loved and needed, so they can better accept the new marriage. Children can't compete with the new marriage partner. Set aside dates and bedtime appointments to sit with the children.

6 | Corporate Staff Meetings Are Mandatory

Many times, throughout the life of Sheridan House for Boys and Girls, we find ourselves in the position of hiring new houseparents. As a residential treatment facility for teenagers, Sheridan House has to have a staff that's very close philosophically. Each counselor's and houseparent's plan for working with the behavior of these children must be consistent.

Houseparents have a special call to this ministry of living with the children. They become surrogate parents to the young people in their particular home at Sheridan House. Much of the time, houseparents are hired weeks before they actually come to work in one of the homes. This often happens because we are waiting for the actual retirement of the previous houseparents.

These houseparents spend their waiting period thinking through the process of how they are going to work with the children when they come to Sheridan House. Before they arrive, we send the houseparents a manual and a book on our philosophy of discipline. Most of them appreciate the materials but don't feel as if they really need the help. After all, they are going to come and save the children from this rigid program called Sheridan House. They don't really believe there is a need for all this work and the orientation meetings we have to help them become houseparents. They have generally already raised their own children and have done a great job of it.

After their arrival we sit with them in large staff meetings on a regular basis. The program director also meets with them every morning during their first month at Sheridan House. Many times they don't seem to hear much of what we are saying. They want to do a good job, but they have their own way of doing it. It doesn't take long until we find that the whole staff in that particular home are battling each other. The houseparents may mean well, but they are not responding to the children with the same plan used by the rest of the staff. The young people in their charge quickly learn how to make the most of the situation. Without much effort they can break the team apart until the houseparents feel as if the rest of the staff are against them.

I've Come to Rescue You

This is quite often the case in the stepparent home. One person marries another person who has two out-of-control children. He may know very little about child rearing, but he knows a few things that he believes can quickly take care of the problems in the home. He can be a rescuer to this family. Once he comes in with his new rules, order will prevail. Unfortunately, the opposite too often takes place.

Ed and Linda were a classic example. They came for counseling because they found that they were spending most of their time disagreeing with each other on absolutely every issue. It wasn't that way when they were dating, but their relationship had quickly become a disaster after the marriage.

Ed was married before and had been divorced for four years. He had two children by his previous wife, but she had custody of those children. Even though he had children of his own, Ed knew very little about raising children. He didn't believe that could be true since he had been a parent, and after all, his children were even older than Linda's children. He should certainly know quite a bit about raising children. The biology of having children didn't qualify Ed as a knowledgeable parent, however. He had not spent much time with his children when he was married before. When he was honest with himself, he could admit that his most earnest time spent thinking about parenting had occurred since the divorce. He dreamed about how he would handle his children, given the opportunity to do it all over again. He was carrying a lot of guilt.

Linda had two active little boys. They were more than active, they were also out of control. In her postdivorce pain and exhaustion she had done a poor job of establishing a discipline plan for her children.

Ed saw a real opportunity once they got married. By the way he handled her children, he could show his new wife what a wonderful catch he was. He could also help himself find a little sanity in their home by establishing several rules to help the boys behave. He had lived alone for a long time and never had to endure all this noise and running, let alone find his tools left out on the back lawn.

Linda added to this problem by letting Ed take over. After all, she knew that the boys needed help. Maybe Ed would be the answer to their unruliness. All of a sudden, after the marriage, Linda backed out of the way and let Ed take over—for a while.

It didn't take long for both Ed and Linda to realize that they had a problem. When things didn't work the way Ed wanted them to, he became more severe with the boys. The boys then ran to Mom for help and she intervened behind Ed's back. "It's okay, boys, he just doesn't understand you yet," she would say. "As soon as Dad leaves the house I'll let you out of your rooms."

Ed became more strict and Linda found herself intervening for the boys on a daily basis. This would frustrate Ed until he started verbally attacking Linda. "You're only ruining these two boys. No wonder they're spoiled rotten. Thanks to you they'll never amount to anything," Ed fired at her one day. In her pain Linda responded with, "We were doing just fine before you arrived."

Ed's approach of walking into the life of this family as a one-man drill sergeant hadn't helped anyone. Linda's acquiescence of her parental responsibilities hadn't helped the family either. This step-parenting style hadn't saved the family. In fact, it almost destroyed the marriage.

Take Time

Like the new houseparents and staff at Sheridan House, parent and stepparent have to work together. No one can walk in and save anything overnight. It's not the *plan* that will work miracles, it's the *relationship*—and this takes time.

As I am writing this chapter, a new staff member has joined the Sheridan House team. Duane, our new comptroller, has been spending his first month at Sheridan House learning about our particular financial system. He is an accountant, but that doesn't mean he can arrive and immediately start doing our books. He still needs to take time to learn about the way we handle our finances. Once he has taken the time to learn about us, he will be better able to make suggestions. The process takes time.

That is a primary ingredient in establishing a successful stepparent home. *Time*. Time in a staff meeting where parent and stepparent can talk about the children as well as time allowing the children to respond to the new home. A stepparent doesn't have the opportunity of watching a child grow up and learning his moods or attitudes. A natural parent has years of experience living with a child from birth onward. This gives her a tremendous wealth of knowledge about the emotional makeup of the child. This is a working knowledge that will take the stepparent a long time to acquire, if ever. The fact that the stepparent may never have the opportunity or time to learn to understand a teenage stepchild means he must rely on the in-house expert on that child. That expert will be the child's natural parent.

Have Staff Meetings

The newlyweds need to set time aside frequently to go over the plan of action they want to establish with the children. These staff meetings could be over coffee for fifteen minutes a day and then once a week for two or three hours. I remember Ed screaming, "Three hours! We don't have three hours to sit down each week and talk about this family. We just need to find a solution to this problem and get on with it." What Ed was saying in his frustration was, "She just needs to get out of the way and let me whip these kids into shape." Unfortunately his plan had been a dismal failure because he had not put in the time to learn about what the family really needed.

Time is a matter of priorities. If the family and the marriage are not worth a three-hour discussion once a week, then both will end in failure. Many homes are willing to give at least a half-hour each night to watch the news. That amounts to over three hours a week. It's a matter of priorities.

The staff meetings must be open to the point that no one feels threatened. The rules are as follows:

1. No accusing statements directed at the other party. "If you didn't do it this way," or "You know you let these kids get away with murder."

2. No defensive statements. "Well, the only reason I did that was because you . . ."

3. Set up a plan to deal with specific behavior. "When Billy does this again how should we respond?"

4. Establish a plan that both parent and stepparent are willing to use in the very same way. Parents need to be consistent so that the children won't divide and conquer.

5. Evaluate the plans that were put into place in last week's staff meeting.

6. Talk about each child individually. It will be important for each parent to learn from the other parent's observations of the children.

7. Remember that the purpose of the meeting is to become a team—a stronger unit.

8. The final thing to be discussed is the marriage. "Now that we have talked about how we are parenting the children, let's talk about how we are treating each other." Remember to follow the same rules.

The plan is to become one unit—a strong team. This can be accomplished through staff meetings. It is even more important when there are two or more sets of children in the home. In homes that are blending children as well as parents, staff meetings need to be even more frequent. This family configuration is discussed in a future chapter.

Every couple means well when they get married. When things don't go exactly as they had planned they have several options. One is to revert to past habits. For some that may mean giving up and leaving: "I did my best, but this family is impossible to help, so I might as well leave and find some other lady who will appreciate my help." Actually that husband never gave it a chance. He may have never taken time to work as a team member.

Another approach may be to get even tougher. By becoming more rigid, with tougher rules, a stepparent may think it's his job to set up a plan of discipline for everyone, including his new wife. This is very dangerous and bound for disaster.

Ed was about to adopt a third approach. He was going to quit and stay. "Linda, these are your children. I give up. There's nothing that can be done with them, and you don't seem to want my help anyway. We'll stay married, but I will no longer have anything to do with these kids."

At that point Ed and Linda came for help. Through staff meetings at home they began to understand each other better. Ed began to understand the children and Linda saw that, though Ed had been overbearing, he was only trying to help alleviate a problem. The staff meetings allowed them to compromise and work toward a plan that would help the children. Actually the staff meetings did much more than help the children have better parents. These weekly meetings helped Ed and Linda learn to love each other more.

"At first I didn't like the idea of these staff meetings," Ed admitted. "I was real uneasy about them and only did it because I knew we were desperate. It wasn't easy for me to admit I might be wrong about some of the things I was doing. Now I realize how important it is for us to have a time to talk. I have to laugh. At first I thought we'd never be able to make it talking for an hour without attacking each other. It was drudgery. Now we sometimes sit out on the porch and talk for well over three hours. It's not only helped the kids, it has helped us."

Staff meetings are a must. There is no way for a couple to get married and then overnight think they can work together with the children. There is no way two people can automatically understand each other, let alone work together in a consistent manner. Without a staff meeting they may never become a team. Linda and Ed had actually become opponents.

Summary

1. It's only natural for the new stepparent to want to put his best foot forward by saving the family. He may mean well by his new rules, but they will only alienate the children and eventually his new wife.

2. Parent and stepparent must commit to sit down regularly (at least weekly) for in-depth staff meetings.

3. These meetings should be used to discuss the children, their attitudes, their behaviors, and how best to deal with the situation.

4. These are not staff meetings to air complaints or make accusations. This is a time to find solutions.

5. Staff meetings should take place at a time when both parents can get to understand each other better and find common ground, as far as a parenting approach is concerned.

6. This is also an ideal time to discuss the marriage, using the same nonaccusing approach.

7. Staff meetings are mandatory if the marriage is to blend successfully.

7 | "Excuse Me, What Do I Call You?"

My brother and I lived with my dad for almost two years before he decided to get married again. As was previously mentioned, my mother had died of cancer while Steve and I were still children. A year after my mother's death Dad began dating a very nice lady, and then they set their wedding date. During their dating period my brother and I spent many evenings with Dad's fiancé and her two daughters. While they were dating we referred to her by her first name, Lisa.

Referring to an adult by her first name was very awkward, but they insisted. When we were first introduced to this lady we quite naturally referred to her as "Mrs. Smith." It was the way we had always been taught to talk to adults. As their relationship became more serious they felt it was not intimate enough to use the word "Mrs.", so they suggested that we call her by her first name.

She was the only adult on the planet whom we brought down to our level and addressed on a first-name basis. Yet nothing else seemed appropriate. I didn't call my teachers by their first names, nor did I refer to any of our adult neighbors by their first names. It was very strange, but it was about to get more difficult.

Then the day came for them to get married. Remember when you were first married and you didn't know what to call your in-laws? Should you use their first names, or finally call them "Mom" and "Dad," even though they really weren't your parents? It can be such an awkward time for many newlyweds, and a time that they avoid calling their in-laws anything. They just talk to them without using a title.

"Hi, this is Bob," rather than "Hi, Dad, this is Bob." The answer to that dilemma comes in one of two ways. The young couple has children and at that point they can title their in-laws, "Grandma" and "Grandpa." By using that title it doesn't seem to infringe on any other family member's territory. It is a true title, since they are the grandparents of the children. Using the title of "Mom" and "Dad" for in-laws is not a true title. They aren't really the son-in-law's parents.

This can be more easily overcome if permission is granted. One day the parents can sit down with their new son-in-law and say, "We are all part of the same family now and we would be honored for you to call us 'Mom' and 'Dad.' " This is the day that permission is granted.

If the situation of figuring out the proper titles is uncomfortable for adults, one can only imagine how difficult it is for children. When a new stepparent comes into a home, it is hard for the child to know what to call him or her. One ceremony takes place and the adult's role changes from being a friend of the child's parent, to that of a stepparent to the child. Overnight from friend to parent. It's no longer appropriate to call this new person, "Mr." or "Uncle." Neither is it correct to make this the only adult the child refers to on a first-name basis. It creates a dilemma for the child.

I remember sitting at the dinner table shortly after my dad's marriage. I was getting ready to ask my new stepmother to pass the potatoes as they were on the table in front of her. As I started to refer to her to ask her to pass the potatoes, I stopped short. *What do I call her?* It was an amazing situation that I can remember to this day. Instead of calling her anything, I just waited until I caught her eye, so I didn't have to give her a title. When she looked over at me I then asked, "Would you please pass the potatoes?" Thus I temporarily avoided risking the wrong title.

A Permission Must Take Place

This is not an unusual area of difficulty for children in blended families. Shortly after the marriage the parents must sit down with the child and help them deal with this problem. "Billy, we want to talk to you about something. Please sit down, Son." This is a conversation that should include both the natural parent and the stepparent.

"It may be awkward for you to know what to call me since your mom and I got married last weekend," the stepfather could begin. "I want you to know a couple of things. I will never attempt to replace your dad. He will always be your father and that's good. In this home, however, I am fulfilling the role of a father. I would be honored for you to feel free to call me 'Dad.' You don't have to if you don't want to, but I want you to know that it would be fine with me. In fact, it would be more than fine, I would be honored. Yesterday when one of your friends came over and I answered the door, I noticed that you didn't really know how to introduce me. Feel free to refer to me as 'Dad' if you like. It's totally up to you."

Answering a Deeper Question

This does much more than give the child permission to call the stepparent "Dad." It answers a question about the whole blending process. Many children wonder if they are just excess baggage in the whole marriage process. One young person said to me, "I always wondered whether I was in the way. When Mr. Jackson married my mom, I had the opinion I was one of the unwanted extras who came along with the deal."

When a stepparent is giving the child permission to refer to him as "Dad," he is also saying that he wants to play a part in the child's life. No, he might not be there to replace the child's natural father. He does want to be a very significant part of the child's growth, however. "You see, Billy, I didn't just marry your mom. I married the whole family." The child needs to be helped to see that he is not in the way where this new marriage is concerned. In fact, he is wanted to the point where the new adult is giving him permission to use a title of endearment.

This needs to be a permission rather than an edict. For many children it might seem that they are betraying their natural father to call this new man "Dad." On the other hand, the child might be yearning for the opportunity to call the man "Dad" and have the privilege of an ongoing father-son relationship. It could be something he might even have prayed for and yet how does he balance it with his desire to be a good son to his natural father? This is true especially if the child has those guilt feelings discussed in previous chapters.

Mom Can Help

This is a situation that needs to be left up to the child. Give him time to think about it after the permission has been given. He can be given one other thing that will help, however. Once the conversation on permission has taken place the child can be given some time with Mom to discuss it.

One mother told me that this led to one of the most wonderful talks she and her son had ever had to that date. "We talked with the children at the dinner table and then that night I sat on the bed alone with each of the children. It opened up the doors to many of Joel's questions. I also encouraged him to talk out loud about his thoughts on referring to his new stepfather as 'Dad.' It was just a great conversation as he realized that it was totally up to him. He also needed to realize that it didn't mean we were going to cut him off from his natural father."

This very wise mother gave her child the opportunity to process the information. So many things were brought to mind by permission. Some negative things such as: "Will this alienate me from Dad?" "Will I be a bad son if I call this new stepfather 'Dad'?" "If I do this will they try to stop me from seeing my dad?" "Why do I feel guilty about this whole conversation?" The child needed help dealing with and talking about this new situation. The best person is often a listening mom (or the natural parent who is present).

The good message to the child that comes out of this conversation is the fact that the child can feel wanted. "This man says that he's glad I'm here. In fact, I can call him 'Dad.'" It helps to begin the blending process. This is a process that many children fight against simply because they don't know how they fit in.

It Helps a Family Become a Family

It's not only the title of the new adult that we are talking about here. It's also the role this new adult is to play. It is often difficult for a young child to begin seeing a person in the role of a parent when he refers to him by his first name. The family can better function when its members are comfortable with their roles.

The appropriate title or even the discussion of that title will help the child begin defining who this new person is. (A) Is this man an intruder into our family? (B) Is he a new husband for my mom? (C) Is he a new father figure for our home? The answer to this multiple choice question is : (D) all of the above. The new stepparent starts out as an intruder and overnight becomes a new husband. Only with time will he successfully become a new father figure. But that process can be launched by defining the direction that the relationship needs to go in.

Labeling the role "father," helps show the child the direction the family intends to go. "No, we are not intending to ship you out or try to get rid of you. Our intention is to become a family." That is why it helps the family blending process to define these roles.

It Will Take Time

Many reading this book will remember how long it took them to become comfortable when referring to their new in-laws as "Mom" and "Dad." This is especially true if your own parents heard you do it. You might have felt that you were betraying the ones who raised you and earned this revered title. The same is true for children. It will take time for the children to risk or feel comfortable referring to the stepparent as "Dad." It will be most difficult to take this risk in front of the other children.

If a child does not take the risk it may be time to open the door for discussion. One parent might want to sit on the child's bed and ask, "I notice that you aren't calling Mike (your stepdad) 'Dad' yet. Is there any reason?" The child may simply feel uncomfortable with using this title, or there may be other reasons already discussed. The important thing is not to force the issue or coerce the child in any way. It would only be significant to give the child the opportunity once again to talk about it.

If and when the child does actually refer to his new stepparent as "Dad" he needs to be encouraged for doing it. Using this title for the first time is a risk and the child needs to be thanked. That would be a great opportunity for the stepfather to sit with the child and say thanks.

"I want you to know that today, when you referred to me as 'Dad,' it made me really proud, Johnny. It will never be my intention to try to replace your own father. But I'm sure proud to introduce you to my friends as my son. I'm proud to fulfill the role of a father in this house. Thanks for calling me 'Dad.' "

This will assure the child that the parent really meant it when the permission was given. It will also help to restate that the stepparent is in no way attempting to usurp the position of the child's natural father. It is a conversation of encouragement that will help the child.

What about Those Who Say "Dad" from the Start?

There are children who begin calling their new stepparent "Dad" immediately. In fact, they title him as "Dad" even before the marriage takes place. By so doing those children may be making many statements. They may be showing how desperate they are for a dad in their life. They may even be using it as an endearing statement to draw the new adult closer to them because they want to be loved.

Some children begin to immediately refer to their new step-father as "Dad" in order to ask a question, "Is it okay to call you 'Dad'?" They are asking whether the new man objects to being called "Dad," or more specifically, if indeed he intends to become a dad to the child.

Just because the child is already comfortable with the title of "Dad" or "Mom" is no reason to avoid the moment of giving permission. The child still needs to know that his new stepparent intends to fulfill the role of being a parent figure in the home. It will still be important to the well-being and security of the child to hear his new family state that they intend to be a family.

Some children refer to their new parent as "Dad" so as to force the new adult into a role. This may be done out of fear on the child's part: "If he doesn't become my new 'daddy,' they may send me off to private school just to get rid of me." Permission to be a family—and an understanding of what roles the new step-parent intends to fulfill—is very important. It will answer many unasked questions in the child's heart.

Summary

1. Children often get caught in the dilemma of not know-ing what to call their new stepparent.

2. Both the natural parent and the stepparent need to sit down with the child and give him permission to call this new adult "Dad."

3. It will be important to help the child understand that this new dad does not intend to replace the child's natu-ral father. This is simply a role that the new dad is ful-filling.

4. This conversation will also help the child understand that he is not excess baggage in the new marital rela-tionship. The new stepparent has married a family, not

just a lady who happens to have kids. This will help the family begin to blend.

5. This time of permission will help the child begin to understand the roles of each family member. The new stepparent intends to be a parent rather than a friend.

6. The process of roles will take time. If and when a child chooses to label his new stepparent as "Mom" or "Dad," he should be thanked. It is a risk for the child and he should be encouraged.

7. Whether the child chooses to use the label of "Dad" or "Mom" for his stepparent should be a decision that is left to the child.

8. The natural parent in the home should make herself available to help the child think through the whole process. It will help the child come to grips with what is happening to his family and indeed his life.

8 | His, Hers, and Theirs

Blending two families takes work, especially when there are many extra facets. Often there is a blending family with an "odd man out." This can make the blending process even more difficult. The odd-man-out scenario takes place when a woman with a child marries and then, as time goes on, the new couple have a baby. The woman's older child can very easily feel like an odd man out.

"Where do I fit in this new, growing family?" This is a typical thought of the older child. It shouldn't surprise anyone to hear that. In other homes, where both natural parents are present, the arrival of a new baby can be a traumatic experience for an older child. The child feels displaced and sad. My own daughter expressed sadness shortly after the birth of her new baby brother. She crawled into my lap and said, "I'm sad because I'm not your baby any more, Daddy."

If this pain is felt in a home where the original or natural family is living together, one can only imagine how alienated a child could feel when his mom and stepfather have a baby of their own. The birth of this new baby is a joyful event that the older child doesn't really feel belongs to him, or so he might think. "Maybe I'm just in the way now," or "I think I want to go live with my father now," are both thoughts that the child might have.

Use the Baby As a Blending Tool

The child in this home needs to be made to feel as if he is part of the process of helping to acclimate the new baby in its new world. The parents in this situation must decide to take the time to pull their older child/stepchild into the family via the new baby. The baby can be used as a blending tool rather than an alienating force.

"Billy, your mother and I are going to have a new baby. This baby is going to be very fortunate to have you for an older brother. I am very grateful that you will be able to help us teach this baby lots of things he will need to know. This baby is fortunate to have three of us loving him instead of just a mom and a dad."

At the very announcement of the baby the older child needs to be drawn into the family process where the new baby is concerned. If not, the child will wonder if he is going to be in the way. Instead, he can be shown that his presence is not only appreciated but even needed.

As time goes on the older sibling should be allowed to participate in some of the discussions about the new life that is about to enter the family. Care should be taken to make the older child feel that he will now be an asset to the family more than ever before. He's a needed part of the team.

Resist the Temptation to Ship the Child Out for the Birth

The time of the birth of the baby can be very important. Many parents will be tempted to send their older child to live with his other natural parent as the birth approaches. Having the child out from under foot may be more convenient, but it is a significant mistake. As difficult as it may be to make arrangements for the child to be present during sibling visiting hours, it is an important part of the blend.

It is extremely important that the child not be sent from his home because of the arrival of the new baby. He won't see the fact that he is being sent to the other home as a matter of logistics. Instead, it could be easily seen by him as the beginning of his alienation. "Everyone is excited about the new baby, but I get sent away. They really don't want me anymore."

When moms and dads say that the older child is truly a part of the team called the family, and then they send the child away for this very important family happening, they show the insincerity of their statement. To send the child away will only further magnify his feelings of being unnecessary and in the way. Keep the older child near you during this special time.

One boy was really made to feel needed by his parents. Joey's mom gave birth to a new little brother and during her stay in the hospital he had the opportunity to have many intimate moments with his stepfather. On the way to the hospital each day this stepfather and son ate meals together in a restaurant and talked about things they were going to do for the baby. The two of them bought a toy that Joey thought his new baby brother would want, and they took it to the hospital. They also spent those few nights at home together helping to get the house ready for the arrival of mother and child. They became a team rather than two people competing for mom. This was a significant time of cementing the stepfather-child relationship.

As time went on and Joey was required to help with the baby, his parents often complimented him in public. "Joey is just an unbelievable older brother for Benjamin. I feel sorry for other kids who don't get to grow up with the privilege of having a brother like Joey." His mom said these words over and over to anyone who would listen.

It's a Negotiation Worth Trying

In many cases it will take planning and even negotiating to make it possible for the older sibling to be able to be in the home during the time of the birth. As so often seems to happen, this event will invariably fall during a time when the child is scheduled to be in the custody of his other home. That may be a convenient excuse to let the child go, but it is avoiding an opportunity. Certainly it's tempting to say to the child, "Well, it's too bad you can't be here for your brother's birth, but you know how important it is for you to visit your father."

Children have seen their divorced parents talk to each other about rearranging visitations for things such as sporting events or special school projects. If this event was as important to the family as the parents are indicating, then surely they would make a few phone calls to see if the child could be with his mom during the birth of the new child. Visitation schedule or not, changes were made in the past when the child's presence was *really* wanted.

If possible the parents who are about to give birth should attempt to get the permission of the other home to allow the child to stay. If the other parent will allow the child to stay, it will show the child just how much he is wanted at the birth. It is an effort and a negotiation worth attempting.

"Joey, I know that you are scheduled to be with your dad this weekend, but I want to ask you something. You know that this is the weekend our baby is supposed to be born. If that happens, do you mind if we ask your father if you can come home to be with us? It would feel strange not to have you with us when such a special family event was taking place."

Talking to the child like this not only gets his permission to shorten his time with his other family, but it also makes a very important statement. His parents show that they want to make an effort to have him with them for the birth. He may not show it on his face but it will be very reassuring.

Blending Families

The term "blended family" is an incorrect label for the home that is putting two families together. The more correct title would be "blending families." This indicates a constant, ongoing process. It will always have its ups and downs. The children in this blending process will spend much of their young lives looking for reasons why the parents are showing partiality toward one of the other children.

The wise parent in the blending home will not be hampered or deterred by the ongoing accusations of favoritism. It is also wise to work hard at avoiding these statements. Using any situation possible to blend the family is smart. The birth of a new baby or another child's soccer game are both events that the whole family can enjoy.

Encourage family members to rejoice over the triumphs of others in the family. Eight-year-old Billy might have a soccer game on Saturday morning. It would be easiest to drop Billy off and pick him up after the game. It would be almost as easy for the natural parent to be the only family member present for the game. Both of those alternatives miss a big opportunity.

This is one more event that can contribute to the blending process. This is the time that the whole "blending family" can make it a point to be present at the game and cheer for its family member. It is an opportunity to teach each person in the family that this new unit is now one, and thus it is important to cheer for each other together.

Blending is not something that takes place simply because people live in the same house. The Stiverson family found that out in a rather painful way. Jerry Stiverson, with no children, married Elaine with a four-year-old daughter, Debbie. After three years of marriage they had a son, Michael.

Many families quite naturally divide up by gender when it comes to the events of the children. Many times this division is even more pronounced in a blending family. It became a habit for Jerry to take his son to all of his events and for Elaine to be in charge of her daughter. This was not always a division of which Jerry and Elaine were conscious. "It was just a habit we got into," Jerry said in the counselor's office. "Elaine had always taken her daughter to everything, and I just figured that I wasn't needed. I guess the fact that I am still calling Debbie, 'her daughter' says something, doesn't it?"

Debbie had not seen her natural father since the divorce—a phenomenon not all that rare when it comes to the female children of divorce. The only father figure that Debbie ever knew was her stepfather, Jerry. Without realizing it Jerry had not worked on the blending process. He had made Debbie feel as if she were not really his daughter. When Debbie became an adolescent her need for male acceptance became acute. Since her dad (Jerry) never seemed as if he wanted to give her any attention she found other males who would. It was for that reason that these two parents came to a counselor for help.

This couple hadn't attempted to blend. After the birth of the baby they fell into patterns that were unhealthy for the blending process. It's easy to do because often it seems more comfortable to divide the children up, either by previous family or by gender. It may be easy, but there will be prices to pay. It will destroy the blending process and make at least one child feel alienated from the family.

The birth of the new baby and the proper handling of this situation is only the beginning. From that point on the parents will have to work hard to see to it that each family member is made to feel that he or she is a significant member of the team. This will take regular, ongoing parental staff meetings. It takes constant stirring to keep paint at the best consistency. The painter can't just stir it once and expect that to last. It's an ongoing, continuous process.

Summary

1. When a couple with a child from a previous marriage have a new baby of their own, they must work hard to make the child-stepchild feel that he is a needed member of the new family.

2. The new baby can work as a blending tool or an alienating force. Much depends on the way the parents handle the birth.

3. The blending process needs to continue long after the birth of a new family member. It needs to continue for the life of the family. This will take a conscious effort on the part of both parents.

4. Often the biggest problem is the fact that dividing the family up is the easiest way to go. The woman takes her children to activities and the man takes his. With that plan the home will always house two separate families rather than one blending family.

9 | "It's Not Fair, and I'll Tell You Why"

That's not fair—Mom always liked you best!" Many comedians have received laughs using this line. It's not just comedians who use this phrase, however. It has become almost a national obsession. People are quick to proclaim, "It's not fair!"

Children in every home are quick to use the it's-not-fair defense. They don't have to be in a blending family to point out that a parent is responding in a manner that shows partiality. Whether the child can justify the accusations or not is irrelevant. It's at least worth a try.

Sometimes in a blending family, however, the children are right. In an attempt to avoid the difficulties of the blending process, it is often possible that the parents aren't being fair. In homes where there are children from different previous families, it is natural for parents to attempt to overcompensate.

The coach for my son's soccer team has his own son on the team. No one had to tell me who the coach's son was or even if Allen was his son. It was easy to see by the way the coach handled him. The coach was far more strict with his own son than with any of the other boys. For the slightest infraction he would pull his son from the game and have him sit on the sidelines. I'm sure when the boy looked at his dad/coach, he said, "Dad! Everyone else is doing the same thing! Why am I the only one sitting on the sidelines?" And I'm equally sure that his father responded with,

"Because you're my son, and I expect more from you than I do from these other boys."

The child was right—it wasn't fair. Not only was it not fair, but he was being punished for being the man's son rather than for his behavior. In a home where two families are attempting to blend, this kind of approach is common. It may even seem logical, but it's not. This parental response only separates the two blending families.

In the coaching situation, at least when they walk off the field the boy gets his dad back. Off the field he is no longer used as an example in front of the other boys. The boy was no longer used as a way for the father to vent his anger at the whole team.

In the blending home, however, the family never walks off the field of play. They will always remain a family. If one parent chooses to use his child as an example or treat his child differently than the rest of the children, there is never any relief for that child. He is always in this role. Actually the child feels betrayal more than any other emotion.

Dividing Rather Than Blending

The Smith family was a blending family. One of the behaviors that Mr. Smith had continually discussed with all four children was that there was to be no "rough-housing" in the family room. Mr. Smith even went so far as to define what he meant by "rough-housing." The problem was not in his rule but rather in his handling of that rule.

Mr. Smith would walk into the family room and find all four children wrestling and rolling all over the furniture. Two of the children were his from a previous marriage, and the other two were his stepchildren. That made all four children his, but he didn't treat them as if they were all his. Mr. Smith's natural reaction was to immediately separate the two families and deal with them differently.

"Bobby and Allen, you come with me." Once he had isolated his own two boys, this biological father would continue, "You two boys should know better than this. I have certainly trained you differently, and I'm very disappointed." Mr. Smith went on to handle half of the children one way and the other half (his wife's children) in another manner. It was a strange situation for his boys to deal with. These children were perfectly willing to get on with the blending process, but their dad continually got in the way. He handled their behavior differently.

The children get one of two messages from this. From the way he handles their behavior, by dividing the family in half, the children must assume that they really aren't one family. The proof was the fact that they were still two different families abiding by two different sets of rules. Both families were told the rules, but only one side of the blended family was forced to abide by them.

Another option for the children to contemplate was that Mr. Smith really didn't love the other children as much, because he didn't seem to care as much about their behavior. A child from the neglected side of the family could surmise, *He really doesn't care whether we break our necks or not.*

Treating the children differently, according to whose they are, is detrimental to the blend of the families. It will put a barrier between the families that will be difficult to remove. It will do more than put up a barrier, however. Treating each side of the family differently will cause bitterness between the children. If they are all treated the same way, they become a team. They must face the same system together and figure out how to deal with it. When they are handled in two different ways they become adversaries.

The Lannigans were putting their homes together but, like the Smiths, they weren't handling their rules in a consistent manner. One of the boys, Larry, was from Dad's side of the home. The other two children were from Mom's side. Dad was a very strict disciplinarian and lived by the book. His wife was not.

The children had recently been approached about playing with matches. They were told how dangerous that could be, and that they would be sent to bed early if they were caught playing with them again. That lecture had a ring of reality to it as far as

Larry was concerned. He knew that his dad meant what he said. The other two boys were not used to such a consistent handling of discipline so it didn't even phase them.

Less than a week later one of the other boys found some matches, and all three boys were out in the garage. The boy pulled the matches from his pocket and a little warning went off in Larry's head. He had several choices he could make. One was to walk away and endure their laughter and ridicule for being a baby. The second was to walk away and go tell the parents that the other boys were out there playing with matches. The third possibility was to stay and play with the matches, knowing that he was disobeying.

In this situation he had to choose between his allegiance to his dad or to the new brothers, whose approval he so desperately wanted. Larry chose the latter, and sure enough, they were caught. As was predicted, Mr. Lannigan dealt with Larry in a very severe manner, especially because he was not used to this kind of blatant disobedience from his son.

Mr. Lannigan didn't realize the difficult situation in which he had placed his son. Either way he went, Larry was a loser. The boy was caught in the middle and he couldn't see what the best decision was. Larry had dreamed of having brothers to play with, and he wanted to get close to them. He didn't want to betray them, yet he didn't want to betray his dad either. The clincher was the fact that he couldn't even save his brothers from the consequences of this behavior when their dad found out. There simply weren't any consequences for the other two boys.

The gulf between Larry, his father, his brothers, and their mother reached such a point that they went for counseling. They were like a bunch of islands in the same body of water, and they were drifting farther and farther apart.

One of the by-products of counseling was to help the Lannigans develop an overall behavioral approach. All the children were now going to be dealt with in the same manner as far as behavior was concerned. No more, "Larry, come over here, I want to talk to you." The children were dealt with as if they were one family, blending.

Mr. Lannigan came into counseling with a very interesting comment one day. He said, "You know, there's a remarkable thing going on in our home right now. I see now that for the past two years Larry has been the enemy as far as the other two boys are concerned. They would try to get him to do things with them, knowing that my wife and I would handle Larry differently than the way we would handle them. That made Larry an outsider. He wasn't getting along with me or with Jimmy and David.

"We have started to treat them all the same and there is a new outsider. The outsider is *me*. From time to time I see Larry siding with Jimmy and David, and I see Jimmy and David taking up for Larry. They have become like . . . well, like . . . brothers. I don't even mind that, for now I'm the outsider when it comes to implementing the rules. I can see that it is pulling us all together. It has even made Jimmy and David a feel little closer to me. I can sense it. They have come to know exactly how I'm going to respond. And I'm learning to love them all enough to respond the same to all of them. We're actually starting to become a family."

Don't Think You Can Compensate

Little Larry Lannigan was suffering because he was forced into a position that alienated him from everyone else in the home. The fact that his father was being tough on him while treating the other two children as if they were someone else's responsibility made life miserable for Larry.

Many times the parent who is acting tougher on his own children, attempts to find ways of making it up to them. He knows that it is wrong and feels guilty. Usually the children will help him see that it's wrong with straightforward comments like "It's not fair that I am the only one who's ever punished for playing with matches."

"It's not fair," is a common plea-bargaining tool that is often perfected by children. At times they talk as if nothing is fair. It is the wise parent who at least examines the situation when he hears that phrase. Sometimes the children are correct.

Stay Away from Cliques

Out of guilt many parents attempt to make it up to their children by getting them off in the corner and forming a clique. "Look, I'm sorry that I treat you differently but we're a family that has been raised differently and I expect more out of you than I can from them." The use of words or phrases such as "they" and "them" says to the child that the two families are not really blending or not even supposed to blend. In fact, it almost creates an adversarial role between the two families. The child can wonder if this whole thing is a farce or only temporary. Are we really a family like they keep saying we are in public? How long is this thing supposed to last?

Oftentimes stepparents find themselves treating the children differently because they aren't sure of their position or status in the home. The parent is not sure whether he or she is expected to be a parent to the children. If that is the reason, then staff meetings between husband and wife are mandatory. These meetings should be a time of discussing common ground as far as the household behavioral rules are concerned.

This staff meeting and behavioral plan will be discussed further in the chapters to come. Suffice it to say for now that some kind of plan needs to be established that is good enough for dealing with the behavior of all the children in the home. The only compensation that should be made is for the age of the child rather than for the previous last name of the child.

Avoid creating private little times that are solely for the purpose of talking about why one family is handled differently than the other. This will only undermine the blending process. Blending is difficult enough. Don't make it more difficult by sabotaging your efforts.

Summary

1. The behavior of the children in the blending family should be handled in the same way. The children should not be treated differently, according to whose they are.

2. The biological parent should avoid taking his own children off to the side for private talks about the "other family" with whom they are now living. That will only sabotage the blending process.

3. If you treat the "sides" of the families differently, you will only make them enemies.

4. Parents should not think they can treat their own child more severely to make a point and then try to make it up to the child later on in private. It won't work.

5. Handling the child of the blending family in different ways may mean that the parents are not quite sure of what their status is as far as the other children are concerned. This is one more reason for staff meetings.

10 | But What If My Child Needs to Talk with Me Privately?

This all sounds so final. I feel like the blending of two families means I have to abandon my child. After all we've been through together, it seems like this is going to be too hard on him." The concerned parent expressing this comment was correct. Now, after nine chapters of emphasizing the blending process, it may be safe to say that a parent can have special, private times with a child.

The idea of blending two families is really opposite to the way the previously single parent has been thinking. A parent will want to blend his or herself with a new spouse, but to let go of the child and blend a whole family together is another step entirely. After all, prior to marriage she was a single parent. The all-encompassing mode of operation of the single parent was "protection." Keep the child close under her wing and protect him or them from all outside forces. After months or even years of that attitude, blending with another family or another adult will be difficult. A protectionist attitude will stifle the blending of two families. After nine chapters of attempting to make that point, it is now safe to say that the needs of the child must not be thrown out in order to blend. We can't throw the baby out with the bath water.

Each child, especially the child of a previous marriage, needs to feel that he has a special place in his parent's heart. He also needs to have someone to help him process all that is going on in his life. The blending process is going to be difficult, so a listening ear and heart is mandatory.

Eric was nine years old, and his mother had recently married a man with two of his own children. This was a hard thing for young Eric to handle. What initially seemed like fun was now overwhelming. Having these two other boys running through the house every other weekend was difficult for Eric. Equally difficult was the fact that this new man had captured his mother's heart. Eric felt invaded, almost betrayed. He needed to be helped with the blending process, but he also needed to be able to talk about it. Who better to talk to than his mom? She was the person with whom he could share. Mom was also the person he could talk to about the absence of his dad.

Realizing the problem, Mrs. Farmer (Eric's mom) set aside time in the evenings to talk with him. Each night, when Eric went to bed, she helped him get into the habit of talking about his feelings. These times of talking were especially helpful on the nights when his two stepbrothers were with them. Eric went through a very emotional time when the other boys were around.

"I could tell that it hurt your feelings when little Johnny got his way about the television show today. How did it make you feel?" his mom would ask. "Oh, I don't know, Mom," Eric responded, not knowing what to say.

"I could tell by your face that you felt something . . . how did you feel?" his mom probed.

Am I Still Special to You?

These were the times when Eric felt less loved or significant to his mom and new dad. From his perspective the whole focus was on the needs and happiness of the other two boys on visitation weekends. It was only natural to feel that way since he was virtually an only child all the rest of the time. He didn't have to share anything or any time with anyone else except when the two boys were there.

It's not his feelings of having to learn to share that are the most significant thing here. It's the fact that the child has no way of processing these feelings. Very often he doesn't have anyone to talk to about what's going on. He's left to decipher his feelings all by himself.

In decades past, children in this situation had people to talk with. When there were difficult things going on in his family a child had lots of options for conversation. Grandma and Grandpa usually lived in the neighborhood. If not them, there was probably an uncle or aunt handy. He could talk to a relative about his feelings.

Another option to help him clarify his unsettling feelings was his community. The whole idea of community was different in decades past. The people who lived around him played a part in his upbringing. They would certainly be available to talk. In fact, the child probably called some of his adult neighbors by the title of "Aunt" or "Uncle." The child of the past had people he could talk to, to help him know that he was still very special to his mom.

Quite often today's child has no one to whom he is close except his mom. It's often difficult for him to talk to this particular person, his mom. If she is not astute enough to let him talk, then he is left with only one prospect—to figure out what's going on by himself, using a nine-year-old's reasoning abilities.

From Eric's perspective he had done something to displease his mom. There was no other way to figure it out. He must not be as special to her as he thought. Why else would she allow the family to focus so much time and energy on these other boys? Why was she fixing them their favorite meals when they were there—and watching their favorite videos.

It didn't really help that she had explained it was only right to cater to them a little more since they were only there every other weekend. She had tried to explain that she and Eric's new dad were trying the make the boys feel comfortable with the new situation. These explanations were lost on a nine-year-old. It was very simple for him to see what was going on. He just wasn't special to her anymore.

This reasoning, and the pain that Eric was going through, made it important for Mrs. Farmer to spend some private time with him. Obviously this meant time where Eric could talk rather than simply hear explanations for the way things were.

Mrs. Farmer was like most moms. When she heard her son accuse her of favoritism, or of not loving him as much anymore, she became very defensive. When her defensiveness made her feel like an inadequate mom, she responded in the wrong way. Backed into a defensive corner, many moms get dramatic and make it impossible for the child to express his feelings. One mom might get angry at the child. Feeling overwhelmed by trying to please too many people, she just explodes. This explosion is not necessarily directed at the child, but his question brings it out—so she unloads both barrels in his direction.

Other moms respond by getting emotional. Due to the exhaustion and feelings of inadequacy of the whole blending process, the mom simply bursts into tears. It's as if she is saying, "Can't I please anybody? As hard as I try to make this a home, now my own flesh and blood feels unloved."

These may be just the feelings that a mom may have when her child attempts to question her about his position in her heart. Whether that is the way she feels or not, she must work at putting her own needs aside. This is the time to become the next-door neighbor.

Becoming the Next-Door Neighbor Can Be Helpful

"Aunt Elaine," the boy started his conversation. Using the name Elaine was proper as it was this mother's actual name. In fact, she was even an aunt. To anyone observing this child call this woman "Aunt Elaine," however, it would seem very strange. This boy was walking up to his own mother and calling her "Aunt Elaine." It was a private little code that mother and child had worked out together.

When Larry called his mom, "Aunt Elaine," it was his way of saying that he needed to talk to her, but he didn't want to hurt her feelings. Basically he was saying, "Mom, can I talk to you about my mom?" Larry didn't have anybody else to talk to about important things. There were no relatives or close neighbors to whom he could run in a flash when he needed someone to help him understand a decision his mother had made.

This very wise mom had seen the need and developed a solution. When he called her "Aunt Elaine" she would attempt to respond like a more objective, less involved neighbor. She had some prerequisites for this arrangement, however. When Larry came up to her and said, "Aunt Elaine, can I talk to you?" he needed to accept the fact that she might ask if it could wait until later. "Larry, can we talk later tonight, when we will have more time together?" She didn't want to take this arrangement lightly, and she knew that his question or need would take more than just a simple yes or no answer. If they postponed their talk until the evening she could compose herself and attempt to be more objective. It would give Larry the chance he deserved to attempt to express himself.

"Aunt Elaine," Larry would begin. "I don't understand why my mom always gives in to the other children when they . . ." A wise "aunt" will not attempt to respond to that question with a pat answer. "Well, your mother does that because . . ." A wise "aunt" will try to draw the answer out of the child by asking more questions. "How does your mother do that?" or "Why do *you* think she does that when the other kids are at the house?"

Answers don't always solve the problems. Sometimes there aren't any answers to life's difficulties. At other times, answers that seem to make sense to a parent, only seem like excuses to a child. It's not necessarily answers that are important, but the opportunity to talk about it.

The rule of this game was that mom must not get emotionally involved in her responses to Larry's questions. The most valuable thing she was doing was allowing him to talk about it, while gently helping him to see another side of the scenario.

On more than one occasion, while playing this special game, Larry reminded her that she was getting defensive and an aunt wasn't supposed to do that. When Larry said that, Elaine had to choose whether to get even more angry or laugh and try to be more objective. She had to choose to supply her child with the listening ear he needed.

But Who Do I Talk to about Dad?

In young Eric's life there were many times when he dreamed about, or thought about, his biological father. Sometimes these were heart-wrenching dreams of expectation. But then he would wake up. The realities of life would do battle with his dreams of spending time with his dad. Eric, and many other children, have this tremendous turmoil inside and don't know who to talk to about it.

Eric felt that if he talked to his mom it would only make her feel bad again. Every time he mentioned "Dad" in the past, she became upset or angry. So Mom didn't appear to be the right person to talk to about these very important feelings of turmoil.

Another possibility for conversation was his new dad. Could he talk to him about his feelings for and yearning for his biological father? It sure didn't seem possible. If he did, wouldn't it hurt his new dad's feelings? After all, weren't these two dads kind of in competition with each other? Eric felt it was almost better to make his new dad think that he didn't care much about his biological dad.

This is just too much for a little guy to carry around by himself. Not only does he need to talk about these often consuming feelings, but these very feelings could supply a very important bridge. Which parent should Eric be able to talk to about his feelings? The answer is both parents. Eric needs the opportunity to talk to his mother and his new dad.

His mother could help him understand more about his dad. His new dad could lend him a listening ear. This conversation could become a bridge between the boy and his new dad. Eric's wanting to talk with his new dad about something so intimate as his feelings for his natural father would open new doors of trust.

One young man described the value of having a stepdad who wanted to listen to these conversations. "I soon came to realize that my new dad really meant it when he said he didn't want to replace my father; he just wanted to be another dad for me. Being able to spend all those years knowing I could go to this man and talk about the pains of losing my dad from my life—that really helped. It even got to the point that I talked to him more than my mom. He became much more than a stepdad. He became a father to me."

There's an Important Lesson to Be Taught

The key to this whole process is the listening ear. Many parents think the key is to have the answers—and that's not true. There are no answers to many of the questions being asked. The lesson is not so much to find answers as it is to learn to express feelings.

There are many children who have deep feelings of pain and loss but don't know what to do with all this. Many go through life expressing their pain by exhibiting antisocial behavior such as substance abuse or premarital sex. They grow up continuing to express their pain in unacceptable behavioral ways rather than by talking about it. Is that enough to scare a parent? I hope so!

Sheridan House, the private residential treatment center where I have worked since 1974, is full of teenagers who have learned to express their pain with negative behavior. The Counseling Center at Sheridan House is constantly dealing with marriages that are dysfunctional because of a husband or wife who has learned how to express hurt in unacceptable ways.

There is no doubt that the child in this new blending home is going to need time and a listening ear—not three-minute, step-by-step answers. Such a child needs large blocks of time when someone will give him the privilege of allowing him to learn how to talk about feelings. This will have a major impact on the child's future.

But My Child Won't Talk

Some of you who are reading this book feel that all is already lost. "When I sit there at night my child won't talk. I know he is hurting, but I can't get him to talk about it! What do I do?" Remember that it will take large segments of time before he can begin trusting. It's a little risky for a child to trust enough to start talking about feelings that he doesn't even understand—especially when someone the child loves has already abandoned the family. Many children feel that it's too risky to open up to the other parent. They are afraid she may leave too.

Other children have no idea how to express what they feel. Join the club. Learning to talk about one's feelings is very adult behavior. It's also learned behavior. We pay a great deal of money to a lot of people in my profession to help us talk about our feelings. That's probably because parents, in some cases, weren't taking the time, sitting on the side of the bed or on the porch.

Helping a child express the pain that a parent knows is inside the child will require a great deal of time. It may also take helpful comments on the parent's part. "I know that you feel bad about the fact that your father didn't come for you this weekend. I would feel horrible too." Then say nothing, allowing the child the opportunity to continue the conversation. The parent must prove to the child that she really wants to listen. This is done by sitting there.

Proving to the child that a parent has a listening ear is also done by accepting the child's feelings. Many times the child may express a feeling that seems ridiculous to the parent. Ridiculous or not, it is a real feeling to the child. The child must feel free to say what he feels. The parent who responds with a statement like, "Now that's the dumbest thing I've ever heard," may completely close the door to further communications. The child won't feel safe to practice talking about what he feels.

It takes time to help a child learn to express feelings. It's certainly time well spent, however. It's an effort that will go a long way toward helping the family blend and feel like a team.

It's also a time that will help the child mature and become a mature spouse in his own marriage. It's a time that will allow the child to learn to deal with his own feelings in beneficial ways.

Summary

1. Each child needs to feel that he has a special place in his parent's heart. This is especially true in the blending family.

2. The child needs someone to talk to about his feelings. The best person to talk to will be the parent with whom he lives. Chances are, much of the difficulties he is having with his feelings pertain to the parent he is living with. This parent can be a great help.

3. When the child needs to talk about problems in the home the parent should do everything she can to avoid getting defensive.

4. Sometimes the child will need to talk about the dad he misses very much. This is an important time to listen.

5. The key is not to supply glib answers to the child's questions. The key is to supply a listening ear.

6. The whole process will help to teach the child how to express his feelings. Later on this will be very important in his own marriage.

Part 3

Dealing with Behavior
As a Team

11 | Learning to Trust Each Other

Ellen was thirteen years old and very angry. She showed her anger by responding to everyone with a sullen attitude. There were times when it was totally impossible to carry on a conversation with her. If someone were to ask her what she was so angry about, Ellen would say she was angry that her mom had recently married a man Ellen didn't like. Two years ago, before this marriage, she would have said she was angry at the fact that she had to live with her mother and sisters in a little apartment. Ellen would have said she was upset about that particular little apartment.

The truth was that Ellen didn't really know what she was angry about. It was very apparent to her counselor that she was angry that her father had moved out. Ellen, however, didn't know how to express that anger, so she chose to be angry at the world around her.

This attitude gave her the opportunity to shift the blame for everything in life. Rather than accept the responsibility for her actions, she could simply be angry at everyone around her. It was never her fault. The whole game of anger had become a habit. It was her regular response to everything that happened. When she did something she wasn't supposed to do, or forgot to do something that she was told to do, it was never her fault. Ellen would conveniently let her anger take over and blame everyone in her path for her problems.

Unfortunately, Ellen's approach to life had gone a step further. She was beginning to let her anger attack her mother's marriage. Ellen's anger was becoming a cancer to the cohesiveness of the blending family. Her mother and her stepfather had both reached the point where they were afraid to confront her concerning the inappropriate things she was doing. Every time they did confront her, the parents somehow got into an argument about it.

One weekend it all came to a head. Ellen was given permission to spend the night at a girlfriend's house on a Saturday. Because her friend's family would not be going to church the next morning, Ellen was told that she must be home by 8:00 A.M. Consciously or not, Ellen saw to it that it was her stepfather who was the one who told her to be home in time to get ready for church.

Jack, Ellen's stepfather, drove the thirteen-year-old to her friend's house that Saturday afternoon. "What time do I have to be home?" Ellen asked as they were pulling into the friend's driveway.

"Your mother will pick you up at 7:30 in the morning so that you have time to get ready for church."

"Oh, please! Can't I just miss church this one time and stay with Darlene's family?"

Jack responded with, "Ellen, we have already been through this. When you asked us if you could spend the night, we said it would be okay only if you could be ready for church the next day. That question has already been addressed." With that, Ellen stormed out of the car as Jack said, "Have a nice time."

The next morning Ellen's mother arrived at the friend's house at 7:30 to pick her up for church. Ellen wasn't even out of bed yet. When her mother was shown into the bedroom where Ellen and her friend were sleeping, she woke her daughter. "Wake up, Honey, it's time to go home so we can get ready for church."

"Oh, I don't have to go," Ellen responded, "Jack said I could stay here and miss this one time." Ellen's mom was totally unprepared for this challenge. "Are you sure? He never said anything to me about changing the plans."

At this point Ellen brought out one of her most useful weapons. Ellen shot a dart into her mother's heart by saying, "You see, you never believe me." This mother felt in her heart that she should have continued with the course of getting Ellen up, but she took the easier of the two roads. Instead of challenging Ellen, she left and chose to ask her husband why he gave in.

Ellen may have won this little skirmish for power, but there was a much greater battle brewing. Ellen's mother, Dana, returned home without the child. Jack had half expected this whole thing to happen. Dana walked into the house without her daughter, and Jack jumped on her.

"Where's Ellen?" Jack asked, already knowing the answer.

In anger, hearing the sarcasm in his voice, Dana snapped back, "Well, you gave her permission to stay later. You could have told me, you know, so I wouldn't go over there looking like an idiot." At this point they were both ready to explode. Unfortunately, they were not upset at the situation but, instead, at each other. Once again they had allowed the child to put them into positions where they wondered whether they could trust each other. It wasn't the child's fault, it was their own fault for allowing this battle to take place.

Dana knew in her heart that Jack probably wouldn't have gone back on their agreement and given Ellen permission to stay. The main reason that she snapped her accusation at him was because of her feeling of helplessness with her child. She also snapped at Jack because of the sarcastic, even triumphant way he asked her where Ellen was. She felt as if he were really saying, "Where's Ellen? Can't you do anything right?" He didn't say that, but the tone of his voice sure sounded like that was what he meant.

Jack was upset because once again Ellen had been allowed to violate the rules. She had set them up as if to say that she wasn't going to be told what to do by anybody—least of all by Jack. He felt as if Ellen had asked him one more time whether she could stay longer at her friend's house, just so she could disregard what he said.

Don't Get Divided

Both parents were upset by the situation. It had become a common occurrence. Ellen had become very adept at dividing them. They now had two choices as they sought to handle this behavioral problem. One was to work together as partners, and the other alternative was to keep fighting each other. Unfortunately, they had gotten into a habit of choosing the latter of the two options.

"We'll see when Ellen gets home," Jack screamed as he stormed out of the room. Both adults were feeling like failures and they were both feeling rejected by the other. This situation had divided them and they were handling it in a way that would only serve to further divide them. They weren't choosing to trust each other.

Choosing to Trust Each Other

Jack should have said, "I know that you didn't mean to get caught in this trap. I should have told you when I got back from dropping her off last night that Ellen had once again asked if she could stay past church. I'm sorry I didn't prepare you for this situation. I sure saw it coming."

Ellen should have said, "I made a mistake and let her stay. I knew in my heart that you wouldn't have changed the plan without telling me. She always gets to me when she says, 'You never trust me, Mom.' I just want to trust her so badly."

Watch What You Attack

At this point the couple should have *comforted* each other rather than *challenged* each other. Frustration with the situation made them lash out at the best friend they had. Nothing can be gained by attacking. In his classic book *Communication in Your Marriage*, Norman Wright tells a story about an old man who spends his summers living in a cabin on the side of a mountain in Wyoming. One morning the old man noticed a herd of wild mustangs grazing in the valley below his cabin. As he watched, the old man saw a pack of wolves sneak up on the mustangs, getting ready to attack. When the mustangs saw the pack of wolves, they immediately circled up with their heads in and their tails out. As the wolves attacked they were able to kick out in a circle and keep the wolves away. The mustangs worked together and eventually the wolves gave up and ran off.

Later that summer the old man sat and watched a herd of jackasses as they grazed in his valley. While he watched, a pack of wolves came back to see if they could fare better with this herd. The jackasses saw the pack of wolves, and they too circled up. Unfortunately, the jackasses circled up with their heads out and their tails in. When the wolves attacked, they kicked each other and lost the battle.

That's the way Dana and Jack were handling their problem. Instead of attacking the problem they were attacking each other. The more they attacked, the more they showed how little they trusted each other. This lack of trust and constant bickering were destroying their relationship. Trust comes in many forms and it must come in the marriage.

Trust Each Other with Failures

This mom had to decide that she could trust her husband with her failures. Trusting meant admitting that she didn't know what to do. It was difficult for her to admit that she didn't really know how to handle the situation. When she was married before, any time she admitted failure or inadequacy that admission came back to haunt her. Those were the exact weapons that her former husband would use against her. "You know, if you knew what you were doing as a mother we wouldn't be having these problems with the children at school," was a typical comment from her ex-husband. He had heard her say that she didn't know how to handle a situation at school. The very fact that she was asking him for help became a major mistake. He used it as a weapon against her.

It had reached the point that Dana was afraid to admit she didn't know something about the parenting process. Then there was the battle she went through to get custody of the children, having to listen to her former husband do everything he could to prove that she was an unfit mother. Dana had built such a wall that she felt it was safer for her to attack her accusers than it was to admit that she needed help. In the past that only caused her more pain. This mom had to risk trusting her new husband with her inadequacies.

Jack had some trusting to do himself. He had to trust Dana with his inability to fix the problem. Jack was a typical male in that he was "fix-it" oriented. When there was a problem in the family, Jack was prone to give a two-minute dissertation about what should be done. If everybody would just follow his advice then everything would be wonderful.

In reality, Jack knew that he felt inadequate to the challenge. Dana acted like she wanted answers but actually what she really wanted was companionship. Jack also wanted companionship, but he thought he had to earn it by coming in and rescuing this family. He thought that meant having an answer for everything.

Jack had to trust that his wife would still love him, even if he didn't always know what to do. In fact, Jack was surprised to find out that his wife wanted to discuss the problem together rather than be told how to fix it. It was a relief for him to know he could admit that he wasn't sure what to do. Both husband and wife finally had a laugh over the fact that it took him a long time to actually say, "I don't know what to do." Instead he would respond with, "I'm *not sure* what we should do here." Even that was a step in the right direction. It was the beginning of trust—trusting another person with one's inadequacies.

Trusting with the Future

The real trust involved the future. They were both so afraid of failing at this marriage that they tended to sweep any of the problems they were having under the carpet. They would do any-thing they could to avoid conflict. Then the problems built to such a magnitude that there was an explosion. In the explosion, they were blaming each other for the difficulties.

Both husband and wife had to trust in the fact that they were in this for the long haul, committed no matter what. With that kind of trust they could work on the problems together.

It was going to be difficult for these parents to help this little girl with her anger. It was going to be impossible to help Ellen, however, if Dana and Jack weren't willing to work together. They needed to work as one person rather than as two more adoles-cents fighting each other.

What this couple needed to do was stop everything, and talk to each other. They were on the same team. They needed to do this until they were calm. Then they needed to get in the car and go get Ellen. Ellen needed to see her mother and stepfather func-tioning as one loving, yet firm unit.

Unfortunately, that didn't happen in this situation. The triangle only got more firmly developed as Ellen returned home and was put into a position of control as the family dealt with the problem. As the next chapter reveals, it was a process that caused further deterioration within the family structure and the marriage. This was all due to a lack of trust. Ellen had chal-lenged her mother to trust her, and that was one of the things that led to the incident. In reality, Ellen was partially right. However, she was talking to her mother about a trust in the wrong direction. Ellen's mother needed to learn to trust her own instincts. She knew she should have told her daughter to come home. This mom needed to learn to trust her new husband. The fact that her previous marriage had destroyed her level of mari-tal trust should not be allowed to destroy this one. Dana needed to trust Jack. Both parents needed to trust their marriage. Scary as that might seem, since they had been hurt in a marriage be-fore, they needed to trust the commitment level of this new marriage. Trust was needed to bond this couple together so they could help their daughter.

Summary

1. Often the weakest link in the blended family is the marriage relationship. That is why it's the marriage that often gets attacked when a home is in crisis. Don't let the circumstances divide the marriage relationship. Strive to work on the problems together.

2. Attack the problem rather than each other. Frustration often causes couples to attack each other. Nothing is solved when this is done.

3. A parent needs to trust his spouse with his own inabilities. One of the beauties of marriage is to be able to share inadequacies with another person. Previously married people often feel just the opposite. They feel as if they will be vulnerable if they show weakness. Parents need to admit it when they don't know what to do about a child's behavior.

12 | The Trial Began

The weekend wasn't over yet for Jack and Dana. The fact that they had not dealt properly with their daughter's challenge to their authority meant there was more battle to come. This mother and stepfather dreaded the moment their daughter returned. They knew it meant choosing sides and going to war. It didn't have to be that way, but that's the way it had always been. Thirteen-year-old Ellen had learned to divide and conquer.

Later on that day, Ellen returned home. She came in triumphantly, knowing that she had gotten her way. She knew full well that they had wanted her back home in time for church. She also knew that her parents' inability to work together would work to her advantage. Though she was aware that a battle was going to take place when she got home, she had already chosen her approach. The technique would be to drive a wedge between them. Ellen would do what she always did—put her parents in a position of attacking each other rather than the problem. She would put them on trial.

All this time her parents had postponed the confrontation until she got home. All the while Jack and Dana were becoming more and more furious at each other. The fact that Ellen was not home, as they had told her to be, was making them furious. What they didn't realize was that deep down inside they weren't really furious at Ellen. Nor were they furious at each other. They were actually frustrated because once again they were in a hole, and they didn't know how to get out. They had not handled the situation like two mature adults.

Ellen was only handling the situation the way she had learned. It was natural for a child to try to get her way. Growing up in a single parent home, Ellen had learned to get her way by attacking her mom. Now that there was a man in the home, the best thing she could do was get them to attack each other. If she were asked, she wouldn't even be able to say that this was what she was doing. By this time it had become a natural approach toward her goal of getting her way.

Ellen walked in the front door right past her stepfather. She was acting as if everything was wonderful. As Jack eyed her over his newspaper, he wondered if this whole confrontation was worth disturbing Ellen's good mood. That thought only lasted a minute, however, as he heard his wife call Ellen into the kitchen.

Jack was determined to stay out of their discussion, so he continued reading the paper. This was a mistake on his part. He thought that it would be better to stay out of the discussion going on in the kitchen rather than end up screaming at everyone. He needed to be in the kitchen giving his wife the support she needed.

Ellen only waited a minute or two before she said something to the effect that nobody really told her she had to be ready for church that morning. At that point Jack threw down his paper and came flying into the kitchen. His anger was so intense that his wife was once again put in the position of judge and jury. Was her daughter right or was her screaming, totally out-of-control husband right.

Once again everybody was the loser. Ellen lost in this situation because she was able to reduce her parents to little more than teenagers themselves. She had no parents to help her get control of her life. Jack and Dana lost because the anger was destroying their marriage and family.

A Better Way

If these confrontations presented such a problem, Dana and Jack should have spent time getting better prepared for the moment of parenting, or in this case the moment of dealing with the rebellious behavior. Dana and Jack should have walked through their plan ahead of time, step by step, so that they would be able to respond in a way that would be constructive.

A better way would have been . . .

"When Ellen comes home how do you want us to handle this?" Jack could have asked. Asking like that would have accomplished much. Unfortunately, in the past Jack had said things such as:

- "Do you want me to handle her? . . . I can take care of this, just say the word. She won't walk all over me the way she always walks on you. Not a chance," or

- "She's yours, you take care of this. Only don't come crying to me when she's totally out of control," or

- "Last time I tried to help you with Ellen it was a waste of my time, so why should I bother?"

Part of the reason Dana dreaded these confrontations was that she was attacked no matter what happened. Being forced into the position of a judge between her daughter and husband was too difficult. If Jack had begun their discussion with a question rather than a sarcastic statement, it would have been very reassuring to Dana.

A statement like, "How do you want us . . . ," would have also shown Dana that they were in this thing together. No matter what had happened in the past, in fact, despite the past, they were going to work on the problem as a team—blending.

If Jack had asked her what she wanted to do, it would have lowered her defenses so that she could have responded with, "I'm not sure what to do. What do you think, Jack?" This would have led them into a staff meeting. "Let's get a cup of coffee and go sit on the porch so we can work this thing out," either one of them could have advised.

It's been said before, but it must be repeated. The perfect answer to the problem is not nearly as important as finding an answer that both parents are happy with. The *blend* is more important than *perfection*. The blend is the ultimate war to be won. Overcoming any and all outside deterrents to the blending process is more important than any individual incident. This little battle that Jack and Dana were facing was only one step in the right direction—a step toward successful stepparenting.

No Screaming, No Attacking

The first step to discussing the confrontation is to talk about the basic form of approach. In other words, the volume level of their voices. Dana would need to say, "I think it's very important that we stay calm as we talk to Ellen. When we yell and scream we don't get anywhere."

This will be the time Jack has to decide how much he really wants to blend. He will know exactly who Dana is talking about. When she says, "We should not be yelling and screaming," she really means Jack. He could get defensive here, or he could get honest.

If honesty prevails, Jack should respond with, "I know what you are saying. I don't mean to get so upset. I guess it's just because I get so frustrated." Otherwise, as they yell at each other, everyone is reduced to acting like an adolescent. Honesty like that would allow both parents to see that they really want to help this child.

Jack should avoid statements of justification such as, "I wouldn't get so upset if you just stuck to your guns." If this staff meeting reverts to another time of attacking, nothing will be accomplished. The only area to which each person should make direct reference is their own areas of difficulty. Dana should refer to the yelling problem as if it was their team's problem. "We should not be yelling."

Where Should the Parent-Child
Discussion Take Place?

The next step is to decide the location of the discussion with the child. Many times parents develop a good plan for dealing with the behavior but they don't really decide where to do it. Without deciding the proper location, they can easily get caught off guard and become frustrated.

The discussion needs to take place in a room or location that can be the most devoid of interruptions. Parents need to make it obvious that they are taking the child and this situation very seriously. They need to give the child their undivided attention. Taking the phone off the hook is also a good idea.

This location, be it the master bedroom, the back porch or wherever, should offer privacy. Many children in a blended home feel as if they must perform for the other children. If there are stepbrothers or sisters listening, the child may be hesitant to respond to the confrontation in a humble manner. Knowing that there is an audience may encourage the child to put on a show. Many times these shows are performed, whether the performer really wants to do them or not. It's all just to save face in front of a stepsister or brother.

Choose a place where there will be privacy. Without an audience the child can more easily choose to act in a natural manner. Many children in blending families want to be parented. They want parents who will love them enough to take control, in a loving manner. That means never embarrassing them in public. Even though they may want a parent who will help them get control of their lives, it is often difficult for the child to relinquish that control. It's humbling. When there are spectators, who are also vying for positions of power, it's even more difficult.

Choose Not to Ask Why

In some situations parents will need to ask why. Most of the time, however, parents already know the answer. If the child were able to verbalize his real motivation for his behavior he would say, "Because I just didn't want to come home when you wanted me to. I created this whole problem for you so I could once again get my way. You know, the way I used to when I was living just with Mom." It does not take a graduate degree to realize that the child will not respond with an answer like that.

When Dana asked her daughter "Why?" Ellen responded by putting the burden of proof back at Dana's feet. "Because you guys said I could." Knowing full well that that was not the case, Dana had asked an unnecessary question. As a matter of fact, Ellen was very prepared for that question. It gave this thirteen-year-old the opportunity to avoid responsibility for her behavior.

Ellen began by saying that her stepfather said she didn't have to come home. Everyone knew that wasn't the case but it didn't matter. The whole room exploded. Ellen then piped in with, "Well, if you knew I was supposed to come home why didn't you just tell me I had to come home instead of waiting until now to fight about this? I wish you guys would get your act together."

Asking why, in this case, was detrimental to the whole process. When a police officer pulls a person over for speeding, he never asks why. "Excuse me, sir, can you tell me why you were speeding down that road?" That's an irrelevant question. He doesn't really care why the person was exceeding the speed limit. The fact is that someone was speeding, and that's against the rules.

Ellen had chosen not to be ready on time. In this particular case, both parents were satisfied with the fact she had been told that she must be ready to go when they came to pick her up. Asking why would only cause unnecessary problems.

During this staff meeting, blending parents must ask the question, "Is there any reason for us to ask why?" The child will make every attempt to tell the parents why, anyway. This will be done because of old habits. When the child, in the single-parent home, was able to establish that it was someone else's fault, he avoided accountability. Don't foster that habit of shifting responsibility. Don't begin the discussion with why.

State the Behavior

It will be important for the parents to be able to state exactly what the unacceptable behavior was. Jack and Dana spent so much time arguing between themselves that it was difficult to establish what behavior they were trying to deal with. Yes, Ellen was late, but was she really late or were the directions that she had been given somewhat confusing?

It will be important for the parents to sit down and establish exactly what behavior they are dealing with. This may be the time they discover that they were somewhat vague in the way they explained the curfew or the responsibility they had placed upon the child. It is a very important time for blending parents to be totally open and honest with each other.

It's easy for parents in this situation to be so frustrated with the child that they don't want to take time to think. They just want to act. The stepparent that wants to blend will ask himself questions such as:

- "Did I really say to her that she was supposed to be in by 8:00?"

- "Was I totally clear in my instructions?"

- "Is there any way that she might not have heard what I said?"

It will be important to establish whether the child could have missed the information. It will be equally important for one parent to trust the other with these recollections. If a parent has truly searched his heart and believes that the directives were clear, the other partner must trust her spouse. The child may do everything in his power to destroy that trust—not because he's a bad child, but because he wants to get his way. This should be repeated: The child is not challenging this whole parenting process because he or she is a bad child. Past habits of battling for control or simply the desire to get his own way are little more than childish responses of rebellion. The child is just showing that he is still a child.

The way to get his way is to make one parent doubt the other. Then he can pass the blame on and avoid accountability. The child who can destroy one parent's trust in another, will do much more than destroy that trust. He could possibly destroy the marriage.

The staff meeting is a time to go over all these details in a calm and loving way, when just the two adults are together. Parents shouldn't wait until their Ellen comes home to talk about the behavior. A constructive discussion is very difficult when the child is present destroying the situation.

The point of this time is to allow parent and stepparent to make decisions together. It's a time to trust each other, a time to blend so as to face the difficulty together.

Summary

1. Parent and stepparent should not wait until the child is present to discuss the child's behavior. Many parents avoid the whole confrontation until they have to deal with it, because the child has returned home or has forced a decision upon them. Parents should find a less volatile time to prepare for the discussion with the child.

2. As a team, blending parents need to discuss how they want to approach the child.

3. Blending parents should select the place that will best allow the child to feel comfortable for the discussion of his or her behavior. It should be devoid of distractions and spectators (brothers and sisters).

4. Blending parents must decide ahead of time that they will trust each other during these discussions.

5. Blending parents must decide to stay calm when talking to the child, or the time with the child will be wasted.

13 | Discussing Consequences

Where the behavior of one's children is concerned, talking about appropriate consequences for inappropriate behavior can be difficult. No family will find this more difficult than the blending family. There are many more variables involved in a blending family that are not present in other families.

Each of the parents has extra baggage to carry when he or she is thinking through possible consequences. A stepparent could find himself trapped in the power game: "I will show this child who is in control of this house." He may be overbearing as he suggests various possible consequences. Worse than that, he may not be *suggesting*, he may be *demanding*.

The natural parent may find herself in a completely different dilemma. She may allow that old, overprotective wave to come over her. Feeling sorry for the child, the mother may want to "let it go this time, but next time I promise that I will do something."

In this struggle to establish boundaries the battle becomes a *marital*, rather than a *parental* disagreement. Similarly, an argument brewed for decades during the taming of the Old West. The farmers wanted to have boundaries and fence off the land. The ranchers wanted no boundaries whatsoever. Their motto was live and let live; no fences, no rules, no one committed to an individual piece of property. The ranchers just wanted to let their cattle run free.

This conflict over the need for boundaries evolved into range wars. Both sides demanded their own way. They refused to negotiate. The fact that they could not come to a compromise over the establishment of boundaries meant that they started shooting at each other.

Stop the Range Wars

Many blending families are going through such "range wars." Parent and stepparent dig into their own opinions of how the child should be raised, and no one will budge. At that point the wars escalate. This is the unfortunate time when many feel it is their responsibility to buffer stepparent and child from each other. The blend is destroyed.

For many years Dana felt that way. The more severe her husband, Jack, was with Ellen, the more lenient she felt she needed to be. Instead of talking to each other and coming to a common plan for structure and boundaries, they just tried to balance each other out. Like two magnets when you put the same poles together, they pushed farther and farther away from each other.

Jack might suggest that Ellen be prohibited from using the phone for a week. Instead of talking about it Dana would say, "Okay." But she would not follow through. Instead, this mom would give in to Ellen's requests to use the phone before the week was up. She would either agree to let Ellen use the phone when the stepfather was not home, or she would pretend she didn't realize that the teenager was sneaking phone calls.

One evening Jack came home and discovered that Ellen was on the phone. It's questionable as to why the daughter chose just that time to place a call, knowing that Jack was due home any moment. Their counselor believed that the teenager wanted to get caught violating the rules—doing something that would force her family to help her be more obedient. It was as if she were asking for help.

When Jack made the discovery, he confronted both his stepdaughter and his wife. It was easy for him to see that his wife was working against him. This only fueled the range wars. Worse than that, it added to Ellen's guilt. Sure, she wanted to get her own way—what teenager wouldn't? Like many children of divorce, however, she carried around a tremendous amount of guilt about the fact that her parents were divorced. It was almost as if she had been part of the cause for the divorce. Now she had a vivid example of the fact that she was "once again" causing her mom to have marital problems. The range wars just heaped more guilt on her. That would affect her behavior in the opposite way from what these parents wanted.

Come to an Agreement

No two people are going to agree upon an appropriate consequence for a child's inappropriate behavior. There are too many different factors involved in the lives of each of the decision makers. The actual decisions become muddied. The biggest problem with this kind of situation is the timing.

When parent and stepparent wait until an incident happens to make a decision about a consequence, they are waiting too long. Once something happens the situation becomes very emotional and tempers tend to rage out of control. Everyone is far too frustrated to be able to make logical decisions.

The best time to come to an agreement concerning an appropriate consequence for rebellious behavior is before the behavior actually takes place. "Wait a minute," Jack asked his counselor when that statement was made. "How can we decide on a consequence before the behavior happens? We don't even know what's going to happen."

"Oh, really?" the counselor responded. "Do you mean to tell me that you fully expected that Ellen would be ready on time? When you discussed the plan with her at home, you expected her to follow through with the plan. When you dropped her off at her friend's house, and she challenged the plan, you still expected her to be ready when you came to pick her up for church early that next morning. Are you saying the fact that

Ellen wasn't ready when she was told to be ready came as a complete surprise?"

Both Dana and Jack looked at each other and dropped their heads. Each knew that this was common practice at their home. They were dreading that Sunday morning, because they knew Ellen would once again challenge their authority. No, they could have planned ahead.

Quality Parenting Means Planning Ahead

Why doesn't the state trooper get frustrated when he pulls a motorist over for disobedient driving? Because he has decided ahead of time what he will do. It's not a situation where he decides as he goes. Before the motorist speeds, the consequence has been established.

Blending parents must use the staff meeting time to make decisions about appropriate consequences before the consequences are needed—before the child challenges the authority of the parents, before emotions begin to flare.

A better way to handle the challenge in question might have been as follows:

Ellen: Mom, can I spend the night at Patti's house tonight?

Mom: I don't know, Ellen. You know that tomorrow is church and Patti's family doesn't go to church.

Ellen: But Mom, couldn't I just miss church this one time?

Mom: No, Ellen. We all need to be in church together. I'll need to talk to Dad about this . . .

Ellen: But Mom, I need to know now or it will be too late.

Mom: Well, Ellen, then you have asked me too late. If you need an answer from me now I'm sorry but I can't answer you.

Ellen: Why do you have to ask Jack before you decide?

Mom: Because Jack and I are married and we make decisions together. Now do you still want me to ask Dad or is it really too late? If it's too late than I'm afraid the decision will have to be no.

Ellen: Okay, ask Jack, and I'll call Patti to let her know later.

That initial communication with Ellen would let her know that family decisions were made by both husband and wife together. This was a new idea to the child, and it was a lesson she needed to be taught repeatedly. Her childhood home didn't function like that. It was an important concept for her to observe.

This approach also gave the mother some time to work through the proper procedure. One other very important point was stressed to Ellen. The fact that an immediate answer was "needed" was not received as the mother's responsibility.

Ellen was attempting to make the apparent urgency of the decision her mother's burden. In reality, this last-minute request was not a responsibility that the mother should have accepted, and Dana didn't. On the contrary, Dana put the burden back on her daughter's shoulders. She basically said to her daughter that there was a decision-making procedure that needed to be followed. If there was no time to go through the procedure, then unfortunately the daughter had waited too long to ask. It was not the fault of the parents, it was the daughter's fault. By waiting too long to ask, she had basically answered her own question.

At Sheridan House for Boys there is a form that all the staff uses to make requests for purchases of items. The forms are used so that the proper procedures can be followed when we are purchasing the things we need for each of the homes. By using the forms we can see to it that we find the best prices possible. Sometimes we can even get the items donated if we have the appropriate time in advance to ask the various businesses. This procedure helps us do that.

All the staff at Sheridan House use these forms very well—except for one staff member. He typically comes running into my office at the last minute saying that he needs new sports equipment for a game that's set to start in ten minutes. "How long have you known that you needed this equipment?" I ask. He responds by saying that he has known that he needed the items since the prior week, when the teams were playing a similar game, but he forgot to fill out the request.

The actual request form takes only sixty seconds to fill out, so I would always do it for him on the spot. Thus he would get his last-minute request. But in doing so, we were defeating the whole purpose of the system. This went on for months. He continued to put the burden of his last-minute requests on my shoulders. "We need it right now. I'm sorry that I didn't ask sooner, but we really need to know now if we can have it." I would always end the conversation with, "Okay, but next time please give us the time we need by filling out the form. Many times we can get the item cheaper if you give me a little time to call around. Next time I'm not going to be forced into these situations."

One day he came flying into my office with several of the boys waiting outside. They were about to take a trip that he had promised them, but he had once again forgotten to make a request for funds. This time I followed through on my statement and turned him down. "What am I going to do?" he asked in shock. "The boys are waiting to go!"

This young man was told he had two options. He could go to the boys and tell them that he had made a mistake and forgotten to go through the proper procedures to get the money to go, or he could pay for the trip with his own money. He was also told one more very important thing. "Phil, you continually come in here trying to make your problem into my problem. Your problem doesn't have to be a problem if you would accept the responsibility to do things properly. It's not fair for you to dump your decisions in my lap. If you want to purchase these things for the children, be responsible enough to do it properly."

This placement of responsibility for one's own actions is extremely important—so much so that an entire chapter will be devoted to it. If the placement of responsibility is not handled correctly it will be difficult for a family ever to blend.

Once Ellen had admitted that an answer was not quite so urgent, Mother and stepfather sat down later to discuss the request:

Mother: Jack, I'd like for her to go, only I want her to be back in time for church.

Stepfather: Then let's let her go, and explain to her that she has to be ready in time to be picked up at Patti's house at 7:30 that morning so we can get her back and get ready for church.

Mother: She won't want to do that. She's already asked if she can miss church.

Stepfather: If we don't want her to miss church, then we really should tell her that she can go to Patti's for the night only if she is willing to be ready to be picked up at 7:30. The choice is hers.

Together Jack and Dana discussed the decision. Together they planned on the way to deal with this request. The most significant thing they did, however, was to place the decision back on the child's shoulders. When they talked to her about spending the night at Patti's and she complained about coming home, they were now better prepared to keep the decision on Ellen's shoulders.

"You just don't want me to go to Patti's house. You don't care about me. You just don't want me to have any fun!" This might be Ellen's typical response when told she must come home earlier the next morning then she wants to.

"Oh, that's not true, Honey," one of the parents can say. "We do want you to go, but we also want you to be with us in church. As a matter of fact, it would be nice if you invited Patti to go, and we'll pick up the two of you. We're not stopping you from going to Patti's. The choice is all yours. You can go to Patti's, but you must be ready for us to pick you up at 7:30 tomorrow morning. Please let us know what you want to do. We will be happy to get up earlier than usual so that we can pick up both of you. You decide what you want to do."

The responsibility for the decision of whether to go or not has been firmly placed in the child's lap. If the child goes, the child is saying that she is agreeing to be ready to be picked up at 7:30. The parents are putting that responsibility on her shoulders.

But What If She Is Irresponsible?

At this point one more area should be discussed in the staff meeting. Ellen will agree to be ready to be picked up on Sunday morning. But what happens if she chooses not to accept this responsibility when the time comes?

This is the time for the blending parents to decide what the consequence will be if Ellen is not ready on Sunday morning. Now—when emotions are not soaring. This is the time when logical, rather than overbearing consequences can be established.

"Wouldn't it just be easier to avoid all this and tell Ellen she can't go?" one parent might ask. Not at all. The parent would be missing a great opportunity to teach the child a great lesson. With this incident, Ellen has an opportunity to learn the concept of personal accountability. She will learn that she is going to be held accountable for something she pledges to do. This learning of that character quality is an essential part of growing into adulthood. Too many people pledge to pay for something when they charge it on their credit card but then have a hard time when the bill comes later. Accountability and responsibility are very important character qualities to learn.

These parents needed to decide what would happen if Ellen wasn't ready to be picked up that next morning. Then during the discussion they needed to tell her.

Parent: It will be fine for you to go to Patti's to spend the night. We will be there to pick you up at 7:30 tomorrow morning. If you're not ready to be picked up tomorrow morning there will be a consequence. We are willing to get up early so that you can do this. But you must be willing to be responsible enough to be ready to go without a hassle. If you are not ready when we come to get you there will be no telephone until next weekend.

Ellen: Oh, that's not fair.

Parent: Certainly it's fair. We're not telling you that you won't be able to use the phone next week. We're only telling you that you won't be able to use the phone if you choose not to use the phone. If you're not ready at 7:30 you will be choosing not to use the phone. You can avoid all this by being ready when we come to get you. We want you to go to Patti's, but we also want you to be responsible about it. It's all up to you.

By doing that the parents placed all the responsibility for the decisions on Ellen's shoulders. The consequences have been established, and she will have to make a choice. She can choose to be responsible or choose the consequence. Everything has been decided in the staff meeting. Everything except the actual handling of the consequence.

Summary

1. Blending parents should make many of their decisions in the nonvolatile setting of a staff meeting.

2. Both parents need to be willing to compromise when it comes to deciding about an appropriate way to handle unacceptable behavior.

3. The best time to decide on appropriate ways to handle unacceptable behavior is before the behavior has taken place.

4. Decide on an appropriate consequence for unacceptable behavior and then discuss it with the child. Place
the decision in her hands. In so doing she will have to
decide whether the behavior is worth the consequence.
She will be learning the character quality of accountability.

14 | For the Sake of the Relationship

One of the most important things to remember when establishing a behavioral plan is that everything is done for the sake of *relationship*. The plan is to help the child grow to a point of accepting responsibility. It is also to aid in the blending process—to help foster the parent-child relationship. Planning ahead, in a less emotional environment, will also help nurture the parent-stepparent relationship.

The placement of responsibility is important. The behavioral plan will not force a child to be perfect. What it should do, however, is put a child in a place where he will be forced to accept responsibility for his own behavior.

Shortly after working with a counselor, Jack and Dana had an opportunity to put a behavioral plan into action. In their subsequent weekly staff meetings they had decided to defer all major parental decisions until they could discuss them together. Their daughter put them to the test very quickly. Ellen asked her mom if she could go to a concert with some friends. This particular kind of concert had been discussed with Ellen in the past, and she already knew that the answer was no. Previous inconsistencies had led Ellen to believe it was worth a try. This time, however, her mother stuck to her guns. The answer was no.

A few days later Ellen came back to her mom with:

Ellen: Patti and I are the only ones in the school who won't be allowed to go to the concert. Since we won't have anything to do that night can I spend the night at Patti's?

Mom: I'll have to ask Dad. We'll talk about it and let you know after dinner.

Jack and Dana discussed Ellen's request and Jack suggested that this time Patti should be invited to spend that particular Friday at their house. When this option was offered to Ellen, it was resoundingly rejected. This sent up a red flag for Jack.

Later that evening Dana and Jack discussed Ellen's request once again. Jack pursued his thoughts with his wife. He asked Dana if she thought there was a possibility that Ellen might be wanting to spend the night at Patti's house only to get a way to go to the concert. "If that's what you think, Jack, then we shouldn't let her out of the house Friday night," was Dana's response.

Then a very interesting thing took place. It almost seemed as if the tables were turned, as far as their handling of Ellen was concerned. Jack expressed the fact that he thought they should let Ellen go to Patti's house. He went on to say that this might be an opportunity to help Ellen learn personal responsibility for her behavior. The whole thing was very difficult for Dana to deal with. Why would they want to let her go, if she might do what she wasn't supposed to do? Why were they going to let her fail?

Jack talked further to Dana about the importance of letting their daughter experience personal responsibility and accountability. Dana simply had to trust Jack and the counselor when they discussed the fact that Ellen needed the freedom to fail.

Together both parents discussed with their daughter their concerns about Ellen's possible motives for spending the night at Patti's. Ellen denied that she was planning to go to the concert. She even acted hurt that they would think such a thing. Then Jack presented the plan:

Jack: I appreciate that you are telling us you won't disobey our wishes for you by going to the concert. We have thought about it, and we've decided that if the temptation gets too great and you do go to the concert there will be a consequence. If you disobey us, you will not be able to go anywhere next weekend. Please remember that next weekend is the big party.

Ellen's head dropped. It was obvious to all that she had indeed planned to disobey her parents and sneak to the concert. Jack went on to explain that he and Dana didn't want to be ogres, but Ellen needed to trust their judgment. Concerts of that particular kind were and always had been off limits.

Then Jack went on to ask a very crucial question: "Now do you still want to spend the night at Patti's? If the temptation is too great maybe you should use us as the excuse for why you can't go." Ellen looked up and said that she still wanted to go to Patti's. All three of them knew that she had made her decision. Live for this weekend and deal with the rest later. Jack finished the discussion this way:

Jack: Ellen we want you to have a great time at Patti's house. I know that you love to go there. But please remember that next weekend depends on your decisions, not ours. We've already decided.

Ellen went to Patti's house that Friday. Jack and Dana did what all parents should do, but unfortunately many are reluctant to do. Dana called Patti's home at 9:00 P.M. to check on her daughter. When she asked to talk to Ellen, Patti's mom said that the two girls were in the pool having fun. She discouraged Dana from having Ellen called to the phone. Dana said thanks and hung up the phone.

At that point she talked to Jack and asked, "Do you think it's possible that Patti's mother would lie to me?"

"Why would you ask that?" Jack asked.

Dana explained the situation and Jack encouraged her to call back in a half hour. When she did, Patti's mom once again said the girls were busy. At that point Dana graciously but firmly stated that she needed to talk to her daughter. As the conversation continued it became apparent that the girls weren't there. Dana confronted Patti's mother, and after a long silence the woman admitted that the girls were indeed at the concert.

The Best-Laid Plans

Hanging up the phone, Dana fell apart. The blending parents sat together trying to decide what to do. Anger made them want to go to the concert and find their daughter. They quickly realized that would be impossible. Their next decision was to go to Patti's house and wait on their daughter. That was a logical decision. They were so furious at Patti's mom that they wanted to call the police.

As they sat drinking coffee Jack said, "You know we have planned for this. We have already established a consequence for Ellen's behavior. She chose to go to the concert against our wishes and we told her what would happen. Why are we all out of control? We need to stay with the plan."

"You mean let her spend the night at that liar's house?" Dana reacted through her tears.

"Later on, when we are in control," Jack said as he reached over for his wife's hand, "we will need to talk to Patti's mom. Right now we would be incapable of doing it in a Christlike manner. I think the damage is done. We should just continue with the course we established when we were less emotional."

The Plan Was Still Not Complete

These two parents had done an excellent job of working together on this crisis. They had blended to form the plan and stayed blended to respond with the plan. This was before Ellen was on the scene to try to break the blend, however. The real test hadn't yet taken place.

Ellen returned home, and they all sat down to discuss what had happened. She was fully aware that her parents knew she had gone to the concert. She was prepared for that. What she wasn't prepared for, however, was the lack of yelling. Jack and Dana were maintaining tremendous control as they discussed with Ellen that she would be going nowhere during the next weekend.

Ellen began to complain about their decision to keep her home. She even tried to shift the blame by complaining that her parents had called to check up on her. "I feel like such a baby! Why do my parents have to go around seeing where I am all the time?" Ellen tried to complain.

Jack was prepared for her complaints. "Ellen, we love you enough to check to make sure you are being honest with us. As long as there is any doubt, we will be checking. As far as the next weekend is concerned, you made the decision about that party, we didn't. We weren't the ones who decided that you couldn't go to the party. You decided to trade the concert for the party. I'm sorry that you made that decision, but you did."

The plan was explained, but it wasn't received well. Unfortunately, many parents think that once they establish a logical plan, the children will respond like mature adults. They almost act as if they expect the child to say, "Oh, okay. That makes sense to me, Mom." Don't expect the child's response to change immediately after a plan has been instituted. The part that will change is this: Now the parent and stepparent are working together.

Blending

The blending of the two parents into one response will make the whole system of dealing with rebellious behavior less volatile. During the discussion the focal point will be much easier to see. The parents are dealing with the child's response to the plan. No longer are they dealing with the child and each other. The stress is significantly reduced. The situation will not get easier until the child believes that the parents are serious about the plan. There will be far less strain on the marriage relationship, however.

As the child sees that her parents can no longer be divided, she will have to make a whole new set of decisions. These decisions are healthy and part of the maturing process. Instead of deciding how to manipulate and separate Mom from Stepparent, Ellen will have to decide whether to obey the rules or not. No longer is it a decision of dealing with the personality of parents. It is now a decision of accepting responsibility for one's behavior. This happens only when the blend of the parents is secure. And that blend is made secure by having a plan and sticking with it.

Ellen walked away from the confrontation a little confused. This was a new approach. She wasn't yet deterred from trying to manipulate to get her way. Nor was she convinced that her parents were able to follow through. But she did see that her parents were no longer arguing with each other about what to do.

As the weekend approached, Ellen did everything in her power to work on her mother. Guilt was the first tactic she employed. Ellen worked very hard to make Dana feel guilty that this was a wholesome party of church kids and now she wasn't going to be able to go.

Dana had been talking all week with Jack about the situation. Once she had even hinted at the fact that maybe, since it was a church party . . . Before she could get the whole sentence out of her mouth, Jack's look made her realize that she was caving in. Sticking to her guns was a new approach for this mom. Together they were going to be able to do it, but it wasn't easy.

As Friday approached and Ellen realized that her ploys weren't going to work, she worked on a new approach to get her way. The amazing thing about this whole dilemma was the fact that Ellen didn't really want to go to the party as badly as she was implying. She just wanted to get her way. She wasn't used to being so powerless where her mother was concerned.

Ellen saved her biggest hand grenade for Thursday night. When she saw that her parents were working together, and that they were going to be consistent she burst forth with, "I've told everybody that I'm going to be there. If you don't let me go to the party, I'm going to ask Dad if I can go live with him."

This was the fear that continually loomed in Dana's heart. She had worked so hard to keep custody of her children. Ellen knew this would be a grenade that would blow their confidence apart.

Respond to the Challenges Calmly

There are several ways that parents must respond to these "Ultimate Challenges." In many cases when a child announces he wants to change custody or the custodial arrangement, the parent can enlist the help of that other parent. A phone call can inform and prepare the noncustodial, or shared custodial parent, of the situation. By doing so, the other parent can be made aware of what is going on.

But in many cases that phone call is impossible because there is no cooperation between the divorced parents. The key to responding properly to this challenge is to keep the responsibility where it belongs. The purpose of this whole plan must be remembered. The purpose is not to keep the child from a party—or even a concert for that matter. The purpose is to keep the responsibility on the proper shoulders.

When a child counters with a threat such as custody or "I'll run away if you don't let me go," the parent must keep the responsibility on the child's shoulders.

Parent: I hope you don't really want to move out of this home. It's your home and we love you very much. In fact, you may not believe this, but we love you so much that we will do everything in our power to keep you as part of this family (or to stop you from running away). You have created this whole problem for yourself and I'm sorry. I'm sorry that you've told your friends that you'll be at the party. I'm also sorry that you won't be able to go to this particular party. I wish you had thought about this when you made the decisions you made last weekend. You made the decision not to go to this party, when you chose to go to the concert. It's not our fault. But I do love you enough to enforce your decision.

Consistently responding in this manner allows the parents to walk away from the confrontation without yelling and screaming. It also reinforces the blend. Equally important, the child is started down the road of learning personal responsibility. No longer can a child get his way by manipulation. He learns that he can get his way by responding properly to the plan. After a while it might even get easy. Accept responsibility for your behavior and you get to go to some of the parties of life.

It was touch and go for Jack and Dana, but they knew that this was a very significant confrontation. Ellen wasn't trying to go to a party as much as she was trying to see if she could get her way. She was pulling out all stops to get her way, while her parents were trying to establish a plan without killing a relationship.

Friday night came, and Ellen realized that she would not be going to the party. Having lost the battle this teenager decided to make life as miserable for her parents as possible. This is when Jack went on the offensive.

As Ellen moped around the house, Jack took out the ice cream. He was bound and determined to have fun. The whole family set up a game to play while they ate banana splits. Ellen refused to be a part of it, though deep inside she was dying to have a bowl of ice cream.

Ellen went to her room, and Jack went the extra mile. He got up from the table and took Ellen some ice cream. She sat sulking in her room, and Jack sat on her floor for a moment to talk. "You chose not to go to the party. I'm sorry that it has worked out that way for you. Part of the punishment does not include being ostracized from the family. We'd love to have you come and play Monopoly with us, but it's your choice. Here's some of your favorite ice cream. We got it just for you. We do feel bad about what has happened and want you to know that we love you."

Don't Allow Yourself to Become the Consequence

Using the plan as they did, Jack and Dana didn't allow themselves to become the consequence. When they used to yell and scream at Ellen, in their frustration, they became the consequence. Without meaning to, they withdrew their love and alienated the child with their yelling. Now there was a consequence that was removed from the parents.

For a while Ellen continued to see her parents as the enemy. She would act as if it were her parents who were denying her the opportunity to go to the parties. After a while, however, she will realize that she is doing these things to herself. If the plan is handled consistently by the parents, Ellen will begin to accept the responsibility for these disappointments.

Best of all, now that the yelling was removed from the plan, Jack and Dana could nurture Ellen. Jack was able to go into the child's room with the ice cream and be on her side. He could show kindness to Ellen without caving in and saying, "Okay, you can go." For a while the child will only see parental kindness if the adults give in to her manipulations.

Relationships cannot be won or lost on whether the child gets her way or not. The relationship must be built through mutual respect. Ellen must be taught personal responsibility while at the same time being part of a family that loves each other. The plan, followed consistently, allows this relationship to grow.

Ellen never came out of her room that night. That was her choice. Jack stayed for only a few moments and then allowed her to have some space. Ellen's mother finished the night by sitting on the side of the girl's bed. As Dana scratched her daughter's back she was able to reassure her of their love. This was not possible in the past because there was no plan. Everyone yelled and screamed so much that no one could stand being in the same room. Now, withdrawal from Ellen was not part of the plan or consequence.

Remind Each Other to Love the Child

Part of the blending process includes reminding each other of the important things. In the past, when there had been a

confrontation between parent and child, Dana just sat and
sulked like her daughter. This mother didn't think that she
could go to her child and love her. She didn't think she could
do that because she was so furious at being manipulated. She
was also oozing with guilt—and her daughter knew how to use
those feelings to get her way.

In the past, mother and daughter had developed a pattern of
staying away from each other after confrontations. This time,
however, the stepparent reminded the parent that she needed to
spend a little time with her daughter. "Remember, we're not the
consequence," Jack said to his wife.

Dana didn't feel like spending time with Ellen at this point,
but she knew that she must—for her sake as well as for Ellen's.
The whole point of establishing a plan is to help the relationship
of the whole family. Now the parents are blending as they work
together to love the child. With this plan everyone wins.

Summary

1. When establishing a plan to deal with the child's behavior, the blending parents must set the limits and
   boundaries before the behavior in question takes place.

2. Blending parents must anticipate a challenge from the
   child. The child will be expecting her parents to fall
   back into old patterns. She may find it difficult to accept this new plan.

3. Above all else the responsibility for the behavior must
   be placed, and left, on the child's shoulders.

4. Once the child challenges the plan he will try to put
   the burden for the decision about the consequences back
   on the parent's shoulders. "Oh, please, Mom. I forgot.
   Let me off this one time."

5. Parents must go through the pain of sticking to the plan
   they have established prior to the incident—before everything got emotional. Don't make the consequence

any more severe just because you are angry. At the same time the parent must resist backing down from the pre-determined plan of action.

6. If the plan is handled properly, the parent will still be able to help the child. Now the parent is not the enemy because there is no yelling.

7. Hence the family is able to blend. The parent and step-parent are working together with a common goal. The child is facing parents who are responding in a consistent unemotional manner.

15 | Recognize the Tornadoes

My grandfather was a farmer. When I was a little boy we spent two weeks on his farm and I will never forget finding "the broken door." "Grandpa, this door has fallen over. It's broken, why don't you fix it?" I asked.

My grandfather went on to explain that the broken door, as I called it, was one of the most important doors on the farm. He told me that it led to the cellar. As he was reaching for the door to show me, I asked, "What's down there, Grandpa?"

"Nothing is down there, Bobby," he said. "This is an important place because we go there for protection when a tornado comes."

As we sat on a bench in the storm cellar my grandfather told me about tornadoes. It was a lesson I will never forget. Tornadoes seem to come when they are least expected and never wanted. My grandfather would work his farm as hard as he knew how, and then a tornado might hit and destroy everything. It didn't cause him to give up. He would just pick up everything that was still usable, and start over again. There was nothing he could do to avoid tornadoes, so he did his best not to get discouraged by the fact that one could come at any time.

"Did a tornado ever hurt the house, Grandpa?" I asked as we walked up out of the storm cellar.

"See that hill way over there by the old well?" he asked as he pointed. "That's where our first house was before a tornado turned it upside down. After that storm we just took what we could from the old house and started all over again. Only this time I picked a little better location."

Tornadoes Can't Be Helped

The previous chapters force me to say that all behavior doesn't lend itself to nice little plans. Behavior can be dealt with, but sometimes children are so committed to the path they have decided upon that their behavior is difficult if not impossible to change without making major decisions.

Blending families have to deal with tornadoes too. No matter how hard the blending parents plan and work together, there will always be the unexpected and unavoidable storms that threaten to destroy the family. It's important to know that many of these storms can't be avoided.

These tornadoes come in all shapes and varieties. Homes that are attempting to blend members of two, three or even more families into one family are going to face outside influences that can cause tremendous turmoil. Some storms come in the shape of noncustodial parents who seem to believe it is their job to undermine the blending family. There are two basic options for dealing with this type of storm: Meet the storm head on vs. Go for cover and ride it out.

Meet the Storm Head On

Meeting the storm head on means the blending family should see if there is a chance to sit and talk with the other family that is influencing a child's life. Brenda and Frank were dealing with just such a difficulty. Ten-year-old Larry was visiting his natural father every other weekend and coming back home with horror stories. Larry's father had a different set of values than his mother, Brenda, and her new husband Frank. Larry was allowed to do things and watch television shows that he was never permitted to see when he was at home. He returned home on Sunday nights bragging to the family—and other children—about what he had done the night before.

This was a tornado warning. The first step was to attempt to set an appointment for a cup of coffee with Larry's natural father. The appointment was set, but it didn't go according to plan. Everyone arrived with his own prepared speech, so that there was no discussion, just yelling. Nothing was accomplished. In fact, it only made the tornado worse.

Fortunately Frank, Larry's stepfather, had the good sense to call and apologize to Brenda's former husband. As difficult as this was, "saving the farm" was more important than standing up to this storm and screaming at it. Another time for coffee was established so that they could talk again about Larry. Even though there was no screaming at this meeting, it became apparent that Larry's father was not going to budge. He didn't see anything wrong with his lifestyle. In fact, he almost seemed to enjoy the opportunity to cause difficulties in their home. It was apparent that he was not going to skip this opportunity to send a storm their way.

Blending couples should not automatically jump to the conclusion that their situation will be the same. Many couples assume that they will face the same wall so they won't bother to try for a discussion. The first step is always to see if there is any possibility for discussing the problem with all parties involved. Don't assume that it's a waste of time.

In many cases the conflicts from the past are so great that communication about the present is extremely difficult. When step one, discussion with the other party involved, has been attempted and has failed, it is time for step two—to go to the storm cellar.

Go for Cover

Many people refuse to accept the reality that there is nothing else they can do. They just spend time arguing about the situation. Others think the storm is fightable. If they just hang in there long enough they can beat the wind. It is very important to understand that there are times to grab your loved ones and head for the storm cellar.

It needs to be said here that going for the cellar, or giving up on saving the farm, should only be done after a tremendous amount of work has taken place. Far too many blending couples give up before they have spent enough time working with a plan to save the family. There are many blending couples that chose to send their child to "live with his father" before they worked at helping the child adjust to his new family. The adjustment (as will be discussed in the next chapter) takes a long time. Parents should be very slow to give up on blending a child into the home. Going for the cellar, or giving up, is only a last resort. This cannot be emphasized enough.

When the situation will not change, acknowledge the fact and do the best you can to cope. When an ex-spouse refuses to help in an area of the child's life, work around it. When a well-meaning, or even a not-so-well-meaning, grandparent constantly interrupts the blending process, talk about it. Once the blending couple has seen that there is little they can do, work around it. It is important not to spend time swinging at the wind. Nothing is accomplished, and this course of action is very exhausting. The blending couple must do the best they can to cope.

When You Go for Cover, Grab What You Can

In the *Wizard of Oz*, when the tornado came, everyone did everything possible to find Dorothy. Remember? Aunty Em didn't want to leave her, so she had to be dragged down into the storm cellar by those around her. They hit a point where they had to close the door, with or without Dorothy. If they didn't, they would not only lose Dorothy, they would lose the whole family. Those are difficult decisions, but sometimes they must be made.

Frank and Brenda hit that point after two more years of battling the storm. Many years before her marriage to Frank, Brenda had worked to get custody of all her children. After her marriage to Frank, Larry never seemed to adjust. Larry was her middle child, and all he talked about was living with his dad. Larry's attitude and determination would be even worse after his weekend visits. Larry's father seemed to be working hard at encouraging this child to do anything he could to get out of the house.

Frank and Brenda were blending five children in their new home. The other children were doing relatively well with this new family. Larry, however, was determined to show everybody that he didn't want to be there. He regularly made statements such as, "This family is stupid. I wish I didn't have to live here." That went a long way toward destroying many of the dinnertime conversations.

Brenda and Frank knew that part of the reason for Larry's attitude was that he didn't feel he was important to the home. Sadly enough, he kept making statements that further alienated him from the blending family. They tried and went out of their way to make Larry feel loved and wanted, but all to no avail. He was bound and determined to create so much havoc that he would get his way.

One night Brenda finally admitted that she didn't think they were going to be able to stand up to this particular storm. As Frank and Brenda were sitting in their bedroom, through her tears she said, "I just left Larry's bedroom and it's the same old discussion. He's begging me to let him live with his dad. I can't believe that I'm saying this . . . but I don't think he'll ever be happy unless we let him go." At that point she began to sob uncontrollably.

This was a decision Frank had come to months before, but he knew he couldn't suggest it. Brenda had to reach this point on her own. She had to work through the fact that letting Larry go to live with his father seemed like giving up. Worse than that, it seemed that she was turning her son out into the storm.

Aunty Em had to realize that she could lose the whole family because one child couldn't be found. It's a tough decision but it often needs to be made. Brenda had to let Larry go to his dad's for the protection of the rest of the family. At this point, after the statement was out of her mouth, Frank had to help her realize that they really had no choice. Larry was going to destroy his own life just to get his way.

Sometimes There's No Cellar

Sometimes there's no answer. One child continually expresses his anger, but there are no apparent solutions. This was the case in my own life. As a sixteen-year-old, I expressed my bitterness over the death of my mother through rebellious behavior. Most of that behavior was vented at my stepmother, though she did nothing to deserve it. There was little she could do, and I made no suggestions. I couldn't say, "Send me to live with . . ." There was no other parent to go to.

That is often the case. A child may scream, saying that he wants to go someplace else, but the sad reality is that there is no other place. Many times the other situation, which the child conceives in his mind, does not exist. Other times there is another parent, but that parent doesn't want the child.

My stepmother made the decision that she would dig in and respond to the situation the best way she could. She went through the motions of raising a blended family of four as if all was well. When my rebellion turned into a tornado, she sought whatever help she could find, established a way to deal with it, and then went on with life. Much of the time I refused to abide by her plan, but that didn't cause her to give up. She just moved on and did what she could to blend the family. She realized that everything can't be fixed. Some things just have to be lived with.

Don't Go to the Cellar Alone

It is very important that the storm not destroy the whole family. My grandfather tried to teach me about the magnitude of tornadoes. When I wanted to know how bad they really were, he told me they were bad enough to cause some people to quit farming. "But those aren't real farmers, Bobby. The real farmers are committed to the land. No matter what happens, after the storm they come out, pick up the pieces, gather what they have and start again. Those who quit aren't farmers, they're surveyors. They survey how hard it's going to be, then they decide if they really want to stay. No commitment. No farmer."

I will never forget those last words. The tornadoes that hit the blending family will cause tremendous stress. Sometimes the decisions that need to be made are extremely difficult. When the tornado turns the house upside down, what happens to the marriage? This is the real land that the farmer talks about. The commitment to the marriage is the significant thing to guard.

No matter how bad the storm gets, the blending couple must do everything in their power to maintain their commitment to each other. The storm will either blow their relationship apart, if they allow it to do so, or it will cause them to work together. The answer to that dilemma is up to the couple. It all boils down to their commitment.

Some couples who begin to blend families are really just surveyors. They want to see if it will work, and they don't really want to have to work themselves. With this lack of commitment, they are sitting ducks for the first tornado: when a child breaks loose and wants to go live with his dad; when an ex-spouse files for the sixth time to take custody away; when the children are expressing pain by fighting the system. All these storms must be evaluated. After the evaluation, the couple must work on what can be changed and accept the reality of the storms that can't be changed. Above all, though, the blending couple must commit to love and support each other through any storm that comes along. The storms should cause them to huddle together in the cellar and hold each other.

Summary

1. All the behaviors that a blending family must face cannot be redirected. Some situations are unworkable and must be seen as such. Many outside influences which come from previous families cannot be avoided.

2. It is important to sort out what can and what can't be changed.

3. Accept the responsibility to change what you can. At the same time, accept the reality that all things can't be fixed.

4. When there are difficulties that can't be overcome or fixed, make sure that they don't destroy the marriage.

Part 4

Becoming a Family

16 | Becoming a Family Takes Time

Several years ago I was in the process of moving across town, from one house to another. In the process of moving I was having a difficult time getting the phone company to understand that I wanted my phones transferred the very day of the move. Working at Sheridan House for Youth meant that the phones were very significant. I felt I needed to be able to receive calls from the staff. Later that week I was talking with my dad about all I had gone through to try to get my phones transferred on the same day. He looked at me and laughed as he told me a story about my grandmother.

My grandmother lived in the mountains of southern Germany. In that part of the world a family has to apply to get on the phone company's waiting list. The wait was approximately two years. That previous summer when her two years were up, my grandmother's turn to get a phone came. Instead of having them install the phone at her house, however, she yielded her position to my aunt and got back on the end of the list. That meant another two years of waiting. More amazing than the two-year wait was the fact that it didn't seem to bother her. She was patient about the process.

What's wrong with today's generation in America? We want everything immediately. It's not only that we want things to happen, but we have come to expect everything to happen now! Our society has raised us to believe that we shouldn't have to wait for anything. If you want it, and can't afford it, charge it. If you want to drive it, and can't afford it now, finance it. If you want to build an addition on the side of your house, don't wait until you have the money—take out a second mortgage. If you want to eat now, don't wait, put it in the microwave. We could almost believe that it's un-American to wait. Have it your way, and have it now. It's surprising that we haven't attempted to find a way to avoid waiting nine months to have a baby.

This kind of thinking often gets in the way of blending two families. Many times couples have come into my office saying, "We just don't think it's going to work with Johnny. We got married a year ago, and he's not adjusting. We're thinking about sending him to live with his father." I wish it was only on rare occasions that I heard these kinds of statements. Not only do I hear it on a constant basis, but I've heard it from couples who have only been married a few months. "We've tried everything with him, and it just isn't working." What they're saying is that it just isn't working fast enough to suit them.

My grandfather would say it's all because we left the farm. For centuries we understood the process of patience. The lesson of patience was built into the agrarian system—*plant and wait*. But while they waited, they did everything in their power to help the process along. The farmer never gave up. Perhaps the fact that today we just go to the store and pull food off the shelf, whenever we want it, has caused us to forget how long it took to get a finished product. Someone had the patience to wait for the harvest.

The Patience Process

Blending parents need to have a certain state of mind. A process is going to take time! The blend is not something that happens at the flick of some imaginary switch or because of a ceremony. It's a process that takes place over a period of time. Never have I seen this understood better than in the blend of the Turlington household. Lila and Bob Turlington married and brought together their two families. Each had a boy and a girl from a previous marriage, making it a blend of six people. Lila's fourteen-year-old son Michael was determined to fight the blend with all the negativity he could muster.

Bob Turlington realized that this young man was doing everything he could to disrupt their new blending family. Bob could recall the night he stood alone on the back porch of their home, fighting the anger. More than that, he was fighting the desire to quit the fight and give up on this new family. Young Michael had once again challenged the authority of the new father figure in the home. Nothing could please the boy and they argued about everything.

"Standing on the back porch, I felt I was losing the battle for our new family," Bob recalled years later as he talked to a support group for blending families. "I was praying and asking the Lord to give me some direction. As I stood there staring off into the night I thought about Moses leading the children of Israel through the wilderness. Like Michael, the Israelites constantly complained about everything. I felt confident that it must have made Moses somewhat depressed also. He must have stood out by his tent at night and looked up at the same stars asking the same God why his 'children' complained so much. I'm sure Moses didn't spend his nights saying, 'Isn't it great that they complain so much? It just blesses my heart to see them so rebellious. Thank You for making them so rebellious, Lord.' No! I'm sure Moses was like anyone else.

"When I began to think about Moses and the fact that he too had to deal with the sullen attitude of his people, it was a help. It was encouraging to see that he never gave up. It was a process for the children of Israel to go through, and the thing that made Moses great was the fact that he hung in there."

Bob went on to say that later on the very same night, he sat down and talked with his wife Lila. She was very nervous that her husband had reached the point of giving up on Michael. If that happened, would he give up on the blending effort altogether? She had seen Bob out on the porch and could tell he was hurting.

Bob told her about his time with the Lord on the porch and how God had brought to his mind Moses and the wilderness experience. They laughed together as he said he hoped his wilderness journey wouldn't take forty years. In fact, he realized that he would only have the "privilege" of interacting directly into Michael's life for another four or five years.

This was a significant day in the life of the Turlington blend. No longer did Lila have to fear for her marriage every time her son attempted to argue about Bob's role. That night Bob realized that the blend would be a long-term process. More importantly, that night Lila realized that Bob was in this relationship for the long haul.

Too often we tend to want to read books like this, or hear speakers who give us four "magical" points, and we believe that we can make the blend take place overnight. The blending process is a time of preparing the soil over and over until we start getting a better and better crop.

The Michaels of the world need to see that this new relationship is permanent and for their own good. They also need to experience a consistent, loving yet firm response from the blending parents, no matter what happens. Slowly, over a period of time, the child or young person will realize that the new family is here to stay. More importantly, he will learn that his parents are responding in the same manner every time. The child will see that it is he himself who is the problem—or causing the sullen attitudes. Then over a period of time he can choose to change and grow into the family. At that point the family may begin to see a more pleasant harvest. It all takes time. It's a process of patience.

Making a Family

If the goal is to blend into a family, it is important to look at what it is that makes a family special. Some in our culture today would believe that a family is little more than people living in the same dwelling who occasionally share a meal together. Actually that sounds more like a dormitory.

In her book *Tapestry*, Edith Shaeffer compares the state of being a family to a child's mobile. When her children were little they would come out of the church nursery carrying metal coat hangers. The hangers would have pictures dangling from strings. Each mobile was supposed to tell a story. Mrs. Shaeffer stated that the family can be easily pictured as a mobile. The people grouped together with the same last name are the hanger. The pictures extending from the hanger represent the experiences that the people have gone through together. They include the happenings that have taken place in their lives jointly and traditions they have developed that help them define who they are. This all contributes to the creation of a vibrant, loving family.

Unfortunately, many families can be represented today by a hanger with nothing hanging down. In fact, many neighborhoods are really little more than closets with lots of empty hangers. Most families today spend little time involved in group activities. Family traditions have just about disappeared. Unfortunately it is the common experience of these events that makes a family special.

Traditions are often the first things that get dropped by the wayside when two families are trying to blend. Whose traditions should they observe during holidays—and with which side of the blending family? Where should they go for Thanksgiving—to which of the multiple relatives' homes? Deciding on what to do about past traditions can become so complicated that families often drop them altogether.

Choose Some Traditions

The best thing blending parents can do is to pick and choose. Talk about past traditions and choose the ones that seem to fit the best. If it has been a long time since there have been any traditions at all, find some together. Realizing that traditions help to make a family special, my wife Rosemary and I have spent many hours poring over the book by Shirley Dobson and Gloria Gaither, *Let's Make a Memory*. It is packed with ideas to help a family create special moments together. We have borrowed many of their traditions and made them our own.

Some families are rich in traditions that are wrapped around special holidays. This can make the celebration of these holidays more significant. One of the reasons some parents drop the "holiday" extras is that their children don't cheer and say thanks. The Michaels of the world say things like, "Do we have to do that?" or "I don't want to do that stupid stuff again." In fact, it is more typical for the children to complain about having to do something extra, like a tradition.

Some time ago Rosemary's family was together and they were talking about the things they did when they were kids. One of her brothers (now an adult) asked why the family never went to hear the "Messiah" anymore. "We always used to do that at Christmas, Mom. Every year you got us tickets, and we went as a family. Actually it kind of ushered in the Christmas season. Why don't you get those tickets any more?"

Rosemary's mom was shocked. She answered her son's question with, "I don't get the tickets like I used to because every time I did it when you guys were growing up, the three of you groaned in agony. It was such a hassle putting up with the complaining that I figured I wouldn't put you through the agony anymore!"

Mrs. Johnson had misread the signs. Yes, they had complained, but it was a tradition to go anyway. In fact, as one of the boys went on to say, not only did they want to go, but it seemed that part of the tradition was to complain about it. Parents need to work hard not to stop doing the enriching things in the family just because the children don't cheer. It's hard to tell by what they say—and it is certainly exhausting to put up with their lack of enthusiasm. However, it is placing the memories on the hanger that makes the family special.

Nonholiday Traditions Are Important

For the blending family, nonholiday traditions are important. In many blending homes the whole family is not together during holidays. It is extremely significant to have times or traditions that help to pull the whole family together so that no one feels like an outsider.

For example, a few Saturday traditions might be Dad's cooking the breakfast so that everyone can gag and act like they are being poisoned! This is a great time for Dad to select one child to be with him as assistant chef. In one house I know of, the dad has gone to the trouble of getting chef's hats and big white aprons so that everyone else can laugh at how ridiculous the two chefs look.

Some blending families are not together on weekends so they have to get creative about their traditions and activities. A game night once a week could be a special way of spending time as a family. There are many things that a family can do on a regular basis that will help them become a special unit. The parents must remember to put the activities on their calendar so that they actually participate in doing them. The most important thing to remember about establishing family activities and traditions is this: *Don't feel defeated when the children aren't excited.*

Does It Get Easier?

One or two experiences of doing something together does not make it a tradition. A tradition is established when an activity is done over and over many times. At a seminar a parent asked, "At what point does it get easier? Do the kids ever stop complaining?"

My first response to that is, "How long did it take them the get the way they are?" It took years for the kids and family to develop the attitudes they have. Likewise, it could take quite a while to help the children develop new attitudes. Again it must be said that the blend is a process rather than an end result.

The attitude of the parents during the process could have a big impact. When the family is participating in a game night the excitement of the parents could be contagious for the children. If the blending parents act as if this is a great time the children could catch on. No one wants to spend a life acting sullen. Sometimes, however, it becomes habitual. When a child or young person has acted sullen for so many years, it sometimes takes time and an excuse to break the habit.

Help Them Break the Habit

Some years ago Ann, a teenager, came to live with us because she was having difficulties at home. To help her feel like a part of our family, Rosemary and I involved her in all our activities. One of the regular activities that we loved was Tuesday-night game night.

On most Tuesday nights Rosemary and I would sit at the dining room table and play games such as Monopoly. When we announced to Ann that we were all going to play Monopoly after dinner she looked as if we had to be kidding. Her first question was, "Do I have to play?"

We let Ann know that we really wanted her to play, and after dinner we set up the table. Ann sat down, stared off into space, and played the game in a very bored and distant fashion. She wanted us to know that she was there but she was not going to have a good time.

We had a basic decision to make. We could say to her, "Okay, you don't have to be here," or we could do everything in our power to help her have fun. It was totally possible that she didn't even know how to have fun without being entertained by an electronic game or the television.

We decided to encourage her to get more involved in the game. I attempted to accomplish that by stealing her money. Ann had her money in little piles stuck halfway under the board. Each pile was a different denomination. Right under her nose I reached over and took the pile closest to me. Ann just stared at me as if I must have made a mistake, but she didn't say anything. A few minutes later I reached over and took the next pile of her money. This time she looked over in shock at Rosemary. Trying not to laugh, Rosemary just went on playing without acknowledging that anything out of the ordinary had happened. Finally Ann blurted out, "What are you doing, that's my money!" To which I responded, "Ann, I didn't think you cared about your money or this game, and I need it to win." Then I just went on playing.

At this point in the game Ann decided to take action. Collecting what little of her money remained, she walked into the kitchen, opened a drawer and got a big rubber mixing spoon. Then she walked back to the dining room table and put her money back half under the playing board. Only this time the money was even closer to me than before.

In moments I reached across to take more of Ann's money. She reached for the spoon and swatted me so hard that she stamped the word "Tupperware" on the top of my hand! I danced around the table, making a fool of myself, and everyone started laughing—even Ann. From that point on there were two games going on. One game was Monopoly and the other was to see if I could catch Ann off guard. The most important thing was that Ann was now participating and even laughing.

I'm not suggesting that you cheat at games to get the children and teenagers involved. It's too hard on your hands! Creativity may be necessary to help the child break the sullen habit. It takes a desire to do whatever it takes to stay with the task of overcoming their difficult attitudes. Above all it takes time.

It's All in the Right Focus

Recently our family had the opportunity to spend a week in the Grand Tetons. One day we decided to walk one of the paths that lead up the mountains. It was amazing how differently we approached this task. I was told that it would take several hours to get to Inspiration Point, so we started out on the walk.

Each step of the way Rosemary and the children wanted to stop and look at the beautiful view. It drove me crazy to stop. I just wanted to get there. They would stop to look, and I would try to hurry them along. Finally Rosemary stopped and said, "Why are we here? Are we here to get to a destination in some record time, or are we here to live each step as we go? It really shouldn't matter whether we even make it to Inspiration Point, especially if we miss everything along the way."

I was so focused on getting to a final destination that I was missing everything in the process. Blending families should be careful of this very trap. It's not the final destination that counts the most. It's not the blend where everyone is one big happy family. The male mind tends to focus on fixing everything rather than living one day at a time. We can miss out on happiness if we think we will only be truly satisfied when the family is "fixed."

It is the getting there that counts. The trip or the process is the thing to focus on. Blending couples should help each other focus on the little step of progress. The blending couples who can be patient with the process and find happiness each day—regardless of whether everything is perfect—these are the families that stand a better chance of building a strong bond. Patience with the process, looking for manna for each day as it comes and never giving up are three important ingredients in the successful blending of two homes.

Summary

1. It is important always to keep in mind that the blending of two families takes time. A marriage ceremony doesn't automatically create a blend.

2. Becoming a vibrant family means more than living in the same house. Blending families need to take time to do things together. They need to establish their own traditions.

3. Blending couples must help each other not become discouraged when the children respond slowly to doing new activities.

4. Focus on one day at a time. An important factor to understand is that it's the process that is important rather than the end result. The end result, the blending of two

homes, will be a lifetime journey. Focusing on today's trip, rather than the destination, will help the parents endure difficult times.

17 | Stepfathers and Sons

Billy was a fifteen-year-old who had spent the past five years of his life in a single-parent home. His dad left the family, and after that Billy had enjoyed very little contact with him during the last five years. Billy deeply desired and dreamed of being more than just a part of his dad's life.

At this point in Billy's life, Jack came on the scene. Billy's mom met and married Jack. This lonely young boy had very high expectations about a possible relationship with this new man in his life. The only problem was that he acted in a way that would indicate just the opposite to Jack. Billy tried too hard and did all the wrong things.

Jack had also dreamed of having a son with whom he could share his knowledge. Beyond that, he wanted to exhibit his love for his new wife by loving her obviously lonely son. But for some reason it was a much harder task than he had anticipated.

When he attempted to tell Billy about something, the boy would act as if he already knew everything there was to know about the subject. Their desire to prove themselves to each other caused them to argue about everything. The harder they tried to get to know each other, the worse it got.

It all came to a head one day. Although the particular event was insignificant, there was an exhibition of tremendous needs and frustration. Boy and man vented their anger at each other.

Learn to Look beyond the Actual Response

It was Saturday and Jack had already announced that the two of them needed to work on the lawn mower together. Jack and Billy were in the garage preparing to change the mower's oil. Man was showing boy how to do the job properly, when Billy piped in and said that he didn't need any help. "I've done this before at my Dad's house," Billy said, sounding indignant. "I don't need you to tell me how to do it."

Jack knew that the boy wasn't telling the truth. And it was obvious that Billy had no idea how to get the old oil out of the mower. They argued for a while, and then Jack backed away, letting the boy start the job by himself, as Billy had requested. Billy found the proper bolt to the oil pan, but when he unscrewed it, he forgot to put something under the mower to catch the oil. At this point the oil spilled out all over the garage floor. Both boy and man became very frustrated. Jack, trying to show Billy the value of taking advice, announced that the boy now had a mess to clean up. Billy, frustrated with the fact that nothing had worked properly, announced that his *father's* lawn mower didn't make messes like this. Further, Billy stated that if Jack would have bought a decent mower this whole mess wouldn't have happened.

At that point the screaming began. Both boy and man lost control and they walked out of the garage in different directions. Each was misreading the other's responses.

The Desperate Needs of Many Boys

Billy wanted to impress his new father so badly that he acted like he knew everything. The only reason he acted this way was because he didn't think he had much to offer. Billy didn't think the man would like him if he really knew what he was like. To avoid dealing with another disappointment, Billy acted like a sullen know-it-all—an impossible way to get to know a new dad.

Many young boys so desperately miss the relationship they dream of having with a natural father that they fantasize. They dream that if their dad would only give them a chance they would be able to show him how wonderful they are. Many times their own dad never gives them that opportunity. The boy never gets to spend any time with him.

In his bitterness, a young boy can assume that nobody will like him—especially a man. As a boy said in my office one day, "After all, if your dad doesn't even think you're worth enough to come and see you, why should anybody else?" Such an experience makes a boy very apprehensive about future relationships with father figures.

Eddie was a young teenager at Sheridan House who missed a relationship with his dad. The pathetically lonely young man had decided on a plan to remedy his problem. He told us that all he wanted to do in the world was to be a professional football player. One day while we were together I asked him why he thought he wanted to be a professional athlete. Without any hesitation he knew the answer: "If I become a professional football player, then everybody will know my name. When everybody knows me, then lots of men will want to be my dad. I'll be able to pick whoever I want. My dad will even want me then."

It was so sad to hear this boy talk as if he were a pet. When the pet couldn't perform, it just wasn't worth having around. If the pet could do lots of tricks then he would be wanted. Eddie could not understand how anybody could love him or even want him around just because he was Eddie. Unconditional love was beyond his understanding.

I Already Know Everything

In some cases, almost as a defense mechanism, a boy often handles a new relationship with two approaches at once. On the one hand, the boy tries to act as if he's a real asset as a son. He imagines he really doesn't need any help, that, in fact, he can teach this new man a few tricks! Fearing rejection, the boy lets everyone know that anyone would be foolish not to want him around. This attitude gets even more difficult to live with when there is more than one son in the blending home. A boy can see the other child as nothing more than competition for "first string." Everything the other child knows is ridiculous or of no value as far as he is concerned. At least that's the way he acts.

Unfortunately many times the boy really doesn't know all the things he acts like he knows. All the things that he brags about knowing turn out to be incorrect information. He can't do all that he claims to be able to do. This causes him even more frustration. As the relationship grows the boy is inevitably challenged by his new father. Even when Billy was challenged in a noncombative manner with the changing of the lawn mower oil, the experience proved to be his undoing. He couldn't go on claiming to know everything, claiming to be great at everything or claiming that his natural dad had everything. These myths will all cave in.

If one child in the home has the ability to make good grades or is a good athlete, then this is the last thing the other boy will want to try to do. He fears that he will not be able to do it as well as his new stepbrother or sister. His typical response will be to act indifferently, as if none of those accomplishments matter anyway. One child's getting positive feedback for good grades can cause the other child to shut down altogether as far as school is concerned.

Sour Grapes

At this point a boy might use his second approach or defense mechanism. To avoid getting hurt again, the boy acts as if he doesn't really care anyway. He exhibits an attitude that is the exact opposite of the way he really feels. The child assumes that he won't be liked or wanted because of his failure to perform.

"I don't want to be a part of this dumb family anyway." That's the way he acts, often alienating himself from things that the family does. In reality he desperately wants to be a part of the family but doesn't know how to go about it. The boy lacks the skills it takes to develop a relationship with the new man in his life. In his tremendous frustration and pain he builds a wall of sullenness that is difficult for the stepfather to penetrate.

Not True for All Children

All children don't respond in such an inept manner. Younger boys may be ecstatic to have a man around to play with, and they will show their enthusiasm. They may come running to their new stepfather with every project looking for approval. They also may be excited to have any instruction they can get, making it easier for the stepfather to feel needed and wanted.

As we noted in a previous chapter, other boys may feel as if they are betraying their natural father if they receive their new stepfather with open arms. In this situation the stepfather must be sure he is not giving the impression that he wants to be a replacement. It is important for the child to view his new father figure as an *addition* to his life rather than a *replacement*.

The Natural Stepfather Response

It is important for the stepfather to gain some understanding of the emotions the boy is feeling. This is difficult when the boy is not able to offer any information. Jack was trying to be a dad to Billy, but as far as he was concerned, it was hopeless. He was interpreting Billy's behavior as rejection. When he came for counseling with his wife he was shocked to hear what Billy's mother was saying. "The saddest thing for me to watch is the amount of misinformation they give to each other," Jack's wife began. "It's so obvious to me that they want a relationship with each other."

At this point Jack broke in with, "I want a relationship with him, but anybody could see that Billy doesn't want any part of me. He acts as if he would be happier if I were dead!"

"Oh, I couldn't disagree more," Billy's mom continued. "In fact, I'd say that Billy wants a father-son relationship with you far more than you do with him. He just doesn't know how to go about it, so you two end up fighting like a couple of children."

Jack's first mistake was that he was misinterpreting Billy's responses to him. He assumed that the boy meant what his words and behavior were saying. Nothing could have been farther from the truth. Jack was so close to the situation that he could not see it for himself. To understand the full magnitude of what was really going on it took listening to his wife for long periods of time and believing her insightful observations. This didn't necessarily need to be done in a counselor's office, but it needed to be done somewhere if the blend was going to begin.

Falling into the Traps

Jack was making another common mistake when dealing with Billy. He was falling into the argument trap. When Billy started arguing, Jack was patient for a while, but he soon reached the point where he couldn't take Billy's attitude any longer. It just irritated him. The arguments would only serve to fulfill Billy's prophecy about his own inability to have a relationship. "Just as I thought," he was saying to himself, "nobody wants to be my dad." There is no way he would ever be able to give any indication that this is what he was feeling. The harder Jack tried to be a dad to Billy, the more frustrated he became. They argued over everything. He didn't want to argue with the boy. In fact, he even spent time talking to himself and praying about the arguments. "This weekend I will not get into an argument with Billy!" But it didn't work. Somehow Billy would find a way to manipulate Jack into some sort of confrontation. The harder Jack tried, the worse he seemed to fail. This went on until it just seemed safer to avoid the boy altogether.

Jack was only looking at the surface. All he saw was Billy's inappropriate response to his friendly overtures. Jack figured that he was wasting his efforts trying to become a father figure for Billy.

And as he watched their relationship slipping away, Billy became desperate. The scene in the garage was typical, but it also appeared to be a final blow. All this had happened because Jack wasn't seeing below the surface.

Two Commitments Are Needed

Dads who find themselves in this trap need to make two commitments. First, they need to realize that they will not be able to control the boy's attitude. Children are often so entrenched in their own pain and feelings of rejection that they cannot be manipulated or cajoled to become positive members of a family.

The dad can commit to his own attitude and response to the new son, regardless of the child's attitude. That is the first commitment to be made. This is an attitude that will necessitate listening to and even soliciting feedback from the boy's mother. Responding the same way requires a significant maturity level. Therein lies an important statement. Jack needed to realize that every time he was falling into argument traps, he was acting like Billy. That meant he himself was acting like an adolescent. "I will love you when you let me teach you," or "I will love you when you let me be a father to you." No relationship works like that. Two people don't start dating and then one day say to the other, "I won't love you until we are married. That's the condition I put on this relationship."

A dad must work at responding to a new son in a loving manner, regardless. The Billys of the world need to be taught how to receive love. The rejection they have dealt with makes it very difficult for them to understand a loving relationship. The son may see a show of love as a sign of weakness—something to take advantage of—all because he hasn't experienced a healthy male-to-male relationship. He's only seen what he thinks it should be in the movies.

Fighting the urge to respond to sullen comments with a suitable retort takes major control. It's called "being an adult." It's important to know that loving the child doesn't necessarily mean *liking* the child. It means teaching the child how love works. Real love is unconditional and consistent—whether at a time when discipline is necessary or when responding to obnoxious attitudes.

The Boy Desperately Needs This for Adulthood

It's all practice for the child's future. Boys will need to know how to respond to other authority figures in their lives. They will also need to know how to love their own sons. When a past father-son relationship has been damaged, a new, growing, mature role model can help teach him the things he needs to know before he steps out into the world. It can also help heal some of his hurts by filling some of his voids.

Second Commitment Is Time

One statement has been repeated over and over in this book: Blending is a process! Just as it took time for a boy to get to the place where he is hampered by so much pain from the loss of a father relationship, it will take time for the child to learn it is okay to let down his guard and just be loved. Each time the stepfather argues with, berates, or ostracizes the boy, the healing process is set back significantly.

It is important to know it may take a long time. It is equally important to know that the process may never happen while the child is still living at home. But it must happen at some point. Some stepfathers have been wise to continue to give the child encouragement long after the boy has become an adult. This affirmation has gone a long way toward helping the boy become a man.

It takes a mature stepfather to avoid feeling intimidated by a teenage boy who thinks he knows everything. A wise stepfather will not allow himself to be placed in a position of competing for his wife's applause. A smart wife will not put her husband in a position of competing for the leadership role in the home. Competition and other immature verbal games will only serve to hurt the boy further, even though he may be the one who causes the games to happen.

The goal should be for the husband and wife to work as a team to develop the boy. This is done with encouragement, unconditional love, understanding, and time—time spent listening to the boy when he doesn't really know what he's talking about. It means simply lending him an ear. The relationship is further developed by doing things such as going to ball games together or showing up to watch the boy play in Little League—all the father-son things the boy has dreamed about doing, even though he certainly didn't act like it. Patience with the process will be a key for the blend to take place. With the help of his new wife the stepfather should assume he's wanted even if the signs aren't there.

Jack Summed It All Up

Jack did the support group a favor by explaining how his wife had helped him develop a new approach for dealing with Billy's attitude. After much discussion between husband and wife, the opportunity came the very next Saturday after the lawn mower incident. Stepfather and Son were working together on another project. They had purchased a swing set for the younger children that had to be assembled. Jack, being a stickler for reading directions, had announced that they really had to sit down and go through the manual first. Billy, anxious to get started with the project, announced that he had "put these things together many times before." Billy added that only stupid people had to read directions.

It was starting all over again, and Jack could feel another battle building. This time he decided that the swing set was not as important as Billy. "Billy," Jack began, "every time we do a job, I automatically act like the boss and that's not fair. This time I'm going to work for you. You tell me what to do, and I'll do it."

One thing Jack did not do was challenge Billy's statement that he had done these things before. He did not say, "Okay, if you're so smart and don't need these directions, you show me how to do it." Jack didn't manipulate the situation so that Billy would never be able to refer to the "stupid directions." All he did was assist Billy as he worked on the project and let the boy think through it.

"It took us eleven hours to complete the job instead of three. Throughout the whole day the younger children kept coming out and asking why we weren't done yet. I was tempted to say, 'Because Billy has to do it his own way,' or 'I don't know, ask Billy.' Fortunately I had enough sense to say that we were both working as fast as we could."

Jack went on to say that Billy was finally able to ask for some advice. As they began, they put some pieces together that looked hilarious and were obviously in the wrong place. They were both able to acknowledge that perhaps they had made a mistake. They were even able to laugh about it. It was the first time they had ever laughed together.

After eleven grueling hours the set was assembled. When everyone came out to see the finished product, a stepfather was able to announce that Billy did it and Jack only helped by doing what he was told to do. "I lost several hours that day, but it was the beginning of our relationship," Jack recalled. He reassured the group that there were still months of relationship difficulties that they had to work on, but his new son now began to feel that he was somebody in the home. Jack summed it all up: "I just had to realize that the relationship was more important than getting the job done my way."

Summary

1. In many stepfather-son relationships there is constant fighting and arguing because they don't really understand each other's needs.

2. Many stepsons are so desperate to be loved and accepted that they are obnoxious or even angry.

3. Many times a stepfather interprets these attitudes as a lack of interest in the relationship. Just the opposite is true.

4. The stepfather needs to work hard at seeing beneath the surface of the boy's motives. He can do that better with the help of his wife. This means that staff meetings are important. After all, who knows the boy better than his mom?

5. The stepfather must commit to giving the child unconditional love (not necessarily "like") by avoiding the arguments over petty things and by spending quality time with the boy.

6. Once again: It is important to know that it took the boy a long time to develop his attitude, so it may take time for him to overcome it.

18 | Stepfathers and Daughters

One of the most difficult relationships in a blending family is the relationship between the stepfather and daughter. At the beginning of this chapter I must confess that I am overly sensitive about some of the more severe difficulties that exist in many of these relationships. At Sheridan House for Girls, our residential program for teenage girls, we have had to deal with countless sexual difficulties between girls and their stepfathers. That is certainly not an issue in the majority of blending homes. Unfortunately, however, it exists in far too many blending families in our society today.

Stepfathers must have an awareness of the fact that sexual identity is a very real issue in the life of an adolescent girl. There are needs that girls ten years and older deal with. This is an age in which the young girl is beginning to work through who she is sexually. It is a significant time for her to be hugged and have her hand held by her dad. It is a time when she has a need to be held and to feel protected by the dominant male in her life.

For many years our society was led to believe that divorce would have a minimal effect on the young female child in the home. This was to be especially true in the home where the mother gained custody of the girl. Research has shown the opposite to be true. There are often very evident differences between the behavior of the daughter of divorce and girls raised by both natural parents.

To cite some of this research one could look at the work of Laurence Steinberg (*Child Development*, 58:1, 1987). He found that girls who spent part of their childhood in father-absent homes were much more susceptible to peer pressure than other girls. In their desire to please, they turned to peers rather than their female parent. Even more dramatic was the landmark research of Stern, Northman, and Van Slyck (*Adolescence*, 19:74, 1974). This in-depth study found that there were far fewer controls in the lives of girls from father-absent homes than there were in the lives of other girls. This research indicated that girls from father-absent homes were not only more sexually active, but also became active at an earlier age. It was also shown that this group of girls had higher drug and alcohol involvement than did other girls.

This is not the result of a few studies but rather the findings of many studies. Girls desperately need a father figure in their lives as they go through the throes of finding out who they are as a young lady and woman. Without the father figure as a boundary-setter, protector, and responder to this need, the young girl is often forced to make many decisions on her own. This once again points to the perfection of God's plan for the family; that is, ideally, the presence of both parents in the home.

No Boundaries

Several things take place in the life of the preteen and teenage girl in a single-parent home. As with other girls she begins to have more social decisions to make. In many single-parent homes, Mom often goes through a period of adjustment during which she is overwhelmed by life. With all the responsibility she must take on, Mom has her hands full meeting the minimum requirements of running a home. One of the areas that often falls into disarray is the area of boundaries for the child.

Mom is often too exhausted to go through the continual battles taking place between mother and daughter. In many cases the preteen and teenage girl battles her way to freedom. Without the presence of a parent who is able to be an authority figure, the girl is free to choose her own activities and constantly push for more freedom.

In this setting the child often pushes the boundaries to the limit and experiences many things that adults should not even be experiencing. All this is done by the child as a quest for approval. She is looking for affirmation from someone and is willing to accept it from anyone. Dad is no longer there, and Mom is too busy and overwhelmed. This leaves her peers as the main mode of affirmation. Pushing for freedom to go and experience new things often gains her the attention she craves from various peer groups.

There is a sad reality that takes place in the lives of many of these girls. It's not really the new experiences that they seek. Many girls have told me that they actually keep pushing for this freedom with the hopes of finally forcing someone to jump in to help them set boundaries. Consciously in some girls, and perhaps subconsciously in others, they are attempting to force a parent to take notice. Their behavior is saying, "Hey, I need you! Please get it together and help me grow up!"

When a parent still doesn't respond, the peers become the boundary-setters of her life. Whatever her peers deem as acceptable behavior she uses as her boundaries for her actions. The peers with whom she usually finds herself are peers dealing with similar struggles. They too are often in the dilemma of living life without much parental input.

Beyond parental boundaries there is also the issue of approval. This teenage girl has a tremendous need for encouragement and approval from someone significant in her life. The fact that she is entrenched in a battle with her mother over behavior makes it difficult for her to reach for or receive approval. Once again she turns to her peers. She can at least gain their approval with very little effort.

Struggle for Sexual Identity

Several years ago a song called "The Men in My Little Girl's Life," was popular. This song was right on target as it talked about the gradual transfer of the girl's hand from father to husband. This is an emotional process that takes place over a period of several years. It was also a song that brought tears to many dads as they listened to it.

One of the roles of a father is to be a protector during the girl's sexual development and awareness. As was previously mentioned, the father, being the primary male in the preteen's life, has the opportunity and privilege of helping the girl grow in a healthy environment of male-female identity. As she has the need of male touch, the father is there to go for walks with her, hold her hand, give her a hug. All of this is healthy, nonerotic, physical contact. Any woman will testify to the great need for this special relationship of protection between father and daughter—especially those women who grew up in homes where they did not receive it.

The girl in the father-absent home has the same needs, but her paths to meeting those needs are often different. Searching for the key to the male-female relationship, she once again finds answers from peers or the television. In a society that is sexually oriented, such as ours, she could very quickly believe that the answer to her need can be met by becoming sexually active.

Often a girl misunderstands the difference between her need for platonic affection and sexual activity. She also misunderstands the fact that a physical touch from a boy does not demonstrate his desire for a mature relationship. Looking to be touched in an endearing manner, many young girls trade sex for the opportunity to be held. This often starts with provocative clothing. Seeing other girls attempt to look years older by dressing in a sexually provocative manner, she battles her mother to dress similarly. The magic begins when she finds herself getting the male attention that she was missing and wanting so desperately. The next step is to pay the price for that attention by becoming sexually promiscuous.

Enter the Conflict

"It was unbelievable," a stepfather exclaimed one day in my office. "At first I thought I must be wrong about what it looked

like. It looked to me as if every time I walked down the hall my
new fifteen-year-old stepdaughter would sit or pose in a provocative way. We had to ask her to close her door when she undressed,
and yet she seemed to keep forgetting."

The difficulty with this situation was the fact that Arnie
(the stepfather) felt awkward talking to his new wife about his
perceptions. "It looked as if she was trying to be seductive when
I was around. How could I possibly discuss this with her mother?"

Over the years this was the way that this fifteen-year-old had
learned to respond to men. She had watched her mother change
her mannerisms when interesting men were around. Her mother
went from a hassled single mom to an attractive lady. The trans-
formation, when around men, was so evident that consciously or
not the teenager learned to copy it.

In other families teenage girls have been taught that the
only way to get attention is to flirt. Wanting desperately to
transform from child to adult, the flirting becomes very provocative. Her flirting becomes sexually oriented and often sug-
gestive.

The explosion took place in Arnie's home when he treated
his new fifteen-year-old daughter like the child she was. For years
this fifteen-year-old had called her own shots as far as social
events were concerned. She was able to wear down her mother
and get to go to places she should never have seen. Now that
her mother had Arnie as a reinforcement, this teenager was
treated more like the child she was. The fireworks broke out at
that point.

The teenager felt that she had been betrayed by her
mother. Why could she do what she pleased before and now
there were rules? She also felt betrayed by her new stepfather.
Why was he acting the way he was when she had been nice?
The responses she had given to Arnie were behaviors which
he defined as not so much nice as they were seductive. The
teenager had responded in the way she felt would bring desired results. Why was he imposing rules on her as if she were
a child?

Going from Adult Back to Child

The most strained relationship in the blending home is usually this quest for relationship and understanding between the step-father and the daughter. Nobody knows quite how to respond. She desperately wants to be loved and protected, but she doesn't know how to build this relationship. She's not even sure if she is comfortable having such a relationship with this new man in her home.

At the same time she is jealous of the new intimacy developing between her mother and this new man. For the first time in years, she is left out of many things that her mother does. The door between them is closed and locked. This adds tension to the situation.

The stepfather often feels very awkward with the new responsibility of a daughter. One stepfather said in his frustration, "I don't even know what to do with a girl. I've never been around a little girl." Another stepfather talked about the guilt he felt when he showed his new daughter attention. "I have two other daughters who live in another state. I don't get to see them very often. Every time I do things with Barbara's girls I feel a pang of guilt in my heart for my own girls."

Making Decisions that Will Help the Relationship

There are so many dynamics to this particular relationship that must be overcome—and they can be overcome. As was true in the other relationships, a key is the constant, ongoing communication between the husband and wife—what we have called "staff meetings." The two adults in the home must share with each other the burdens about the children, and they must be open in their feelings. If this communication breaks down, little else in the home can be built up.

I realize that it has been stated many times in this book, but it is never more significant than when discussing the dynamics of good stepfather-daughter relationships. Take time to develop the relationship. Many overzealous, well-meaning stepfathers have done tremendous damage to this relationship by being too aggressive.

Little girls must feel comfortable with the new arrangement. Perhaps a better word would be *safe*. A thirteen-year-old at Sheridan House described what safe meant in a beautiful way. When she was talking about her relationship with her stepfather she said, "He made me feel safe because he hugged me, but not too much or too hard. He always knocked and asked permission before he came into my room, and then he made sure the door was left opened. When I asked to go places that I knew they didn't want me to go, he said no, but he always said it was because they loved me and wanted to protect me. I hardly ever acted as if I liked to hear those words, but deep inside it sure felt good. I feel safe with my stepfather because he gave me space and he loves my mom."

Her last statement has always been valuable to me. This girl felt safe and loved because her stepfather gave her space. He didn't overwhelm her or force himself on her as a father. He was gentle yet firm in his decisions. He acted like a father, yet he let her choose whether she was going to love him back.

The best thing he did, however, was to very aggressively love her mom. When I asked him what his formula was, he said something very simple. "I knew my new daughter needed hugs. But I also knew she was very self-conscious about her budding sexuality. I decided to hug her in a very mild way around the shoulders. When I would come up behind her I would softly touch her shoulder with my arm and hand. That way I wasn't in her way. She could walk forward and escape my hug if she wanted to, which she did at first. As soon as she found out it was okay not to be hugged, she rarely walked away. Then she actually wanted the hugs, because she knew she had a choice.

"When I hugged her mom, however, it was full blown. She got to see me give her mom major hugs. That way she knew the difference between marital hugs and parental hugs. I think it made her feel more secure to see us hug each other. The most fun was when my wife and I would pull her into our arms and have a family hug. She would scream that she was being smothered but she sure came back for more."

This was a very wise stepfather. He set boundaries, but he let his daughter know she was loved. She had the privilege of progressing in the father-daughter relationship at her own speed. He was wise not to overpower her. But he was also very wise in the way he demonstrated his love for her mom. He proved to her that this was a new family worth investing in. This relationship wasn't a flash in the pan, it was going to last.

Summary

1. Stepfathers need to move very slowly in their quest to love their new daughters.

2. It is very important to allow the daughter her own space. She may not be ready to have someone sit in her room and talk to her.

3. Touch is very important for a preteen or teenager, but be very careful to allow her the opportunity to move away from a hug.

4. The greatest thing a stepfather can do is love the girl's mother. The stepfather should aggressively demonstrate love to his wife in front of his stepdaughter. It will make her feel more secure.

5. Be aware of all the sexual identity issues with which preteen and teenage girls deal.

19 | On Being a Stepmother

To me it appeared as if she moved in like she owned the place. It had been almost two years since my mother had died. With the stroke of one brief ceremony a new mom moved into our lives and our house. It wasn't that she was rude or bossy, she was just there. For two years it had been my dad, my brother, and I. It wasn't just the three of us any more, and without any provocation on her part, I resented this new step-mother.

There's Something about That Name

There's probably no name that has been more smeared or misrepresented in literature than that of "stepmother." In children's literature she is depicted as an overpowering shrew who immediately begins to try and remove her stepchildren from the scene.

Generally speaking, nothing could be farther from the truth. The function of stepmother is usually very difficult, and that is because of the saintly role she is trying to assume. She is given the task of filling the sacred role of "Mother."

In my case, Mom, having died of cancer, had become a saint in our eyes. All we seemed to be able to remember were the perfect things she did. These were accomplishments that no new step-mother would ever be able to match because they were so glorified.

I felt as if it would be a horrible betrayal ever to admit that any-one could do anything half as well as my natural mom. This made life very difficult for a new stepmother, trying desperately to please the sons of her new husband. The harder she tried to please, the harder we searched for flaws in the things she attempted. She was taking on what seemed to be, at times, an impossible task.

Boys and Their Moms

Boys seem to have a very different and often unrealistic atti-tude concerning their mothers. Years ago at Sheridan House we had a boy living in residence with us whose mother was a prosti-tute. He was very angry with her about the way she lived, and they had previously gotten into many physical battles. As angry as he was, and as nice as the new home at Sheridan House was, he still wanted desperately to go back and live with his mom.

She lived in a broken-down home that was bug infested, but it didn't matter. He wanted to be with her anyway. It took me a long time to realize that he wasn't just playing games. She was his mom and there was a bond between them. No matter what she was like, this boy wanted to be with her.

The Perverseness of It All

Boys have such a special understanding of their mother's love, that she is often the one to whom the boy will choose to be the most rude. Mothers have asked, "Why is it that my son says rude things to me—things that he would never say to anyone else? He's more obnoxious around me than he is when he is with his father."

Many might mistakenly think this difference in behavior is because the father is more likely to respond in a punitive manner to a child's obnoxious behavior. Some might think it is because if he treated Dad the same way he treated his mother, his father would do something about it. That is probably not the only rea-son that a child seems to innately treat his mother worse than he does his father. The most probable reason lies in this fact: A child understands, consciously or subconsciously, that his mother is more forgiving in her love toward her child.

A study by Harris Goldstein (*Journal of Consulting and Clinical Psychology*, 1972) found that fathers tend to be the providers of performance-oriented love. If the child does well, or does what he is supposed to do, the father tends to acknowledge the behavior by letting the child know he is loved and appreciated. On the other hand, the study indicated that mothers are the providers of noncontingent love. No matter what the child does or how he performs, the mother lets the child know he is loved. In other words, the mother's approach to loving her child is saying, "No matter what you do I will always love you." The mother in the family tends to be the person who illustrates "perfect" love.

A child is conditioned to know that he must behave one way for one person, but that he can let his guard down when he is responding to Mom. The fact that he often doesn't treat her as if she is special is his back-handed way of saying he knows she is very special. He takes her for granted because he has been taught that she will always love him. Her love is special enough to last even when he acts immaturely and rudely around her.

Boys at Sheridan House often tease each other with comments that can be very cutting. When one boy is angry at another boy he may say things about personal appearance, or many other possible insults. A new boy had arrived at Sheridan House and before too many days he became embroiled in one of these verbal battles. Several boys were standing around listening and making sure that the two boys never went beyond the point of verbal exchanges. All of a sudden the new boy made a derogatory comment about the other boy's mother. At that point the room became very still and all were looking at him as if he had broken the cardinal rule. He had! Next thing we knew, we were breaking up a fight.

Some very interesting conversations took place after the fight. When we talked with the boy who made the derogatory comment about the other boy's mother, his first statement was,

"The minute it was out of my mouth I knew I had made a mistake. It was like the whole group turned on me."

The boy whose mother had been insulted said that he knew they were never permitted to get physical but, "I had to do something. He said something bad about my mom." He felt totally justified about doing what he did since the other boy had touched "sacred ground" when he brought his mom's name into the battle.

Even more interesting was our talk with the boy's mother later on that week. When she was told that her son had gotten in a fight she was somewhat surprised. But when she was told that the fight was precipitated by another boy saying something derogatory about her, tears filled her eyes. She wasn't pleased that her son had gotten in a fight for any reason whatsoever. She was, however, shocked that he would fight to protect her name. "By the way he acts sometimes, I had gotten to the point that I felt like he thought I was his maid." It shocked her that he cared for or thought of her as special.

Translate That Emotion into a Replacement

Take that very special person away from him and he is dealing with a tremendous loss. In my own life there seemed to be no appropriate way to express this loss except to show unrealistic loyalty. No matter what the stepmother would do to express her love for the family, it was my job to find something wrong with it rather than accept it. I took it upon myself to make life miserable for her.

The Answer to Rejected Love Is Love

The stepmother must realize a very basic premise: She will never be able to overcome a myth, so she shouldn't try. The worst mistake a stepmother can make is to attempt to become the first lady in the lives of her stepchildren. That position may come with time, but it will never be reached by competing. Usually the natural mother, no matter what, is talked about as if she is an untouchable goddess in the eyes of the children. If she is still involved in the lives of the children, this is a position that would probably shock her to hear about. "I wish they would act like I was special when they are around me," one natural mother said.

A stepmother should become her own person, rather than attempt to operate the same way her predecessor did. The children need to get to know her for who she is rather than just see her as someone attempting to copy the real thing.

It doesn't hurt to try to maintain the same routine in the house and attempt some of the same meals or traditions. This can be done just as long as the stepmother is prepared for comments like, "That isn't the way Mom did it" (or "does it" as the case may be).

A stepmother must work together with her husband to come up with a behavioral plan that can be handled in a consistent manner. This plan has been dealt with in previous chapters, but it is very important. For the stepmother who is dealing with the children during visitation or all the time, it is significant to have a very consistent plan that she can follow. The children will learn to understand her better.

It is also important for her to be willing to eventually establish some new family activities and traditions. Lana did that very well when she married Richard. The children had become stuck in their routines and patterns. Having lived with a very pragmatic father for several years, family life had become rather sterile. Life alone with Dad went from chores, to meals, to homework, to bedtime, and that was about it.

Lana decided that there needed to be some effort toward incorporating some family fun into the routine. When she suggested that they play word games while eating dinner, everyone complained. Each had become accustomed to speeding through the meal and back to their own rooms or individual worlds. Even Richard made a sour face when Lana made the suggestion.

Lana then asked for their help. "This is very hard for me too," Lana told them one night. "In the home I grew up in we always played a game called 'Thinking Of.' One person would think of something and the others would try to guess what it was. I kind of miss those mealtime games. I know that you all have important things to do, but if you would just stay a little longer at the dinner table and play this game with me, it would be a big help. It would remind me of when I was a kid."

Reluctantly they all decided to help Lana. They played the game until everyone had a turn at "Thinking Of" and then they left the table without comment. That night when Lana said good night to each child she thanked them for helping her play the game. It would have been easier for Lana to just say, "Forget it. This is too hard." But she didn't want to let them go on as they were. Lana knew it was her job to help the boys out of the doldrums.

For several nights they played the game with Lana always having to be the one to bring it up. Each night someone at the table gave a grunt of complaint. One night Richard even made the very unhelpful statement, "Come on, boys, let's play her game. It's the least we can do since she cooked the meal."

Lana felt as if this was a total waste of time until one night when she got up from the table to walk into the kitchen. They hadn't played the game that night because they were running a little behind. "Wait," one of the boys said, "aren't we going to play 'Thinking Of'?" Lana responded with, "Not tonight, boys, I have to get these dishes ready so we can get to church." To Lana's amazement they began to play the game without her.

That was the encouragement Lana needed to know that if she went slowly, and helped create her own style, the boys would respond. She had to create the family fun asking for help and not expect much direct encouragement. From there the game progressed until the whole family stayed at the dinner table a little longer each night. Sometimes they actually talked instead of playing the game! Lana was helping the boys trust family life again. She was doing it using her own style and yet she was going very slowly.

Stepmothers and Daughters

There is often a very different relationship for boys versus girls, as far as stepmothering is concerned. Though girls are loyal to their natural mothers, they are also more accepting of another person. As with the boys, the process of becoming a family member takes time. Different from boys, the girl may deeply resent the entrance of another "woman" into the house. Due to her special relationship with Dad, this is often the case.

Many girls develop a close relationship with their dads after a family breaks up or the death of the mother takes place. When the father remarries the daughter may feel very threatened. The daughter may have fulfilled the role of the "woman of the house," and now she is being replaced by a new and more competent woman, the stepmother.

The wise stepmother will work hard at not making the daughter feel as if she is unnecessary. The stepmother can help the girl understand that her new presence in the home is really an opportunity for the daughter rather than a replacement. The daughter can be made to feel that she now has a comrade who will understand things Dad didn't understand about girls.

The stepmother can develop a relationship by asking for advice about things such as, "What do you think everybody would enjoy having for meals? What are some of your father's favorites?"

There's a Fine Line

The relationship between stepmother and daughter may develop into a very special friendship. It is important, however, for the stepmother to maintain the posture of an adult. That doesn't mean that the stepmother can't be the center of fun with the daughter. Doing things together that are things friends would do, such as shopping, are fun and necessary. That will build camaraderie.

It does mean this however: that the daughter will have to learn that she is not the number one female in Dad's life. That can be accomplished by setting aside times when husband and wife are together alone—times when a baby-sitter is used or the older daughters stay home by themselves.

Some parents have indicated that they have these dinners when the daughter is visiting her other set of parents. That is a fine and very considerate idea, but it doesn't get the point across. The child needs to see that the marriage relationship is the priority relationship in the home. At some point the child needs to experience dealing with being left out of the couple's life for a few hours during the evening. Otherwise, a daughter may be led to believe that she is the center of the family and that all activities should revolve around her. When this happens discipline opportunities between stepmother and daughter may become family splitters. It's very healthy for a daughter to learn to accept her father as a devoted husband to her new mother. Not only is it healthy, but it will also help her understand more about the marriage process.

Once Again, Time Is Your Friend

Many stepmothers enter the new home and see the situation as a project rather than a delicate balance. Instead of trying to diagnose the situation and the personalities involved, the stepmother can find herself working too fast to add what she has surmised to be a much needed "feminine touch." This can only serve to alienate many of the more insecure children. Dad may like it because he is now freed up to worry about the things in life that he feels more capable of doing.

A stepmother should be careful not to let Dad escape the family. If she takes over he may feel that he has successfully subcontracted the family's needs out to this new female. He may feel he is not needed anymore. Coupled with that is the fact the stepmother will not be allowing herself the opportunity to learn to understand each member of the family. She will simply be attempting to force the family members into molds that she thinks they should fit.

Time is not an enemy; it's a friend. Just as it took time for a woman to understand the man she is marrying, it will take time to learn about the children she is blending with. That process doesn't take place during dating, because everyone is playing a role. They are not responding to life in a natural manner. The children themselves will need time to process their grief. Whether the loss of Mom is due to death or divorce, both cause deep emotions of loss. The children will need the opportunity and even the privilege of dealing with loss. This takes time. It may also take outside professional help.

If a stepmother will take time to understand, to slowly initiate new ideas, never try to compete with the "saint" she is replacing, and then become a friend as well as parent to each child, she will eventually be successful. Success will be defined by having a relationship with the children while feeling comfortable with the handling of structure. My own stepmother found success by waiting long enough to become my "other mom" rather than a stepmother.

Summary

1. The stepmother must understand that she is seen as attempting to replace an unseen saint—Mom.

2. A stepmother must be willing to go slowly and take her time as she develops a relationship with the children.

3. It may take longer with boys as they sometimes think they are betraying their natural mother if they accept her.

4. Daughters may feel they are being replaced as the women of the house. That relationship is also a slow but very worthwhile process.

5. Stepmothers should *slowly* try to institute their own style of "family." That way they can be seen in a different light rather than attempting to compete with the previous mom.

6. Love and patience will eventually change the way the children view the new woman of the house: from a stepmother to "other mama."

20 | No Competition Please

Audrey and Fred pull into the driveway of an all-too-familiar house. It's the home of Audrey's ex-husband and this is their every-other-Sunday-evening routine. They are picking up Audrey's two children from their visitation weekend with their father.

As usual, the children come running to the door of their father's home with squeals of excitement. They are excited to see their mom at the door, but they are also ecstatic to show her all the presents their father has given them this weekend.

Another Disney World Weekend

Audrey says her usual pleasantries to her ex-husband, gathers up the children, and all their new gifts, and they head to the car. The big question is how to respond to the fact that the children have once again been "bought." All weekend, like every other visitation weekend, the children were taken places, bought toys and clothes, and allowed to do whatever they wanted.

It will take two days to get them back into the necessary routine. They have been without boundaries or restraints all weekend. The lack of structure made it bad enough, but added to that was the fact that the children quite naturally found the time with their father much more exciting. They played the entire time with no rules. To them, Dad's house was more fun.

Audrey and Fred had to make some decisions about how to respond to this competition for the love of the children. The children might not want the parents to feel competitive, but that's irrelevant. It is very difficult for one parent to watch another parent shower the children with "candy" and not feel uncomfortable.

A Stepfather's Decisions

Fred had to deal with feelings of inadequacy. There was just no way he could compete with the amount of money that Audrey's ex-husband had to throw around. It was seemingly endless, and being the male that he was, Fred felt that he was not able to provide the extras he would like to give to his new family. "When the children came running from their father's beautiful home and jumped into my old Chevrolet for the drive back to our crowded home, it made me feel small. It got even worse when they told us about all the things that their father bought for them and the places they went. I can hardly afford for us all to go out for a nice meal once a month, and they eat every meal out when they're with him. In my heart, I know I'm doing the best I can. But sometimes my ego gets the best of me, and I am tempted to pull out a credit card and salve my wounded pride. I feel like shouting, 'On the way home let's have dinner and go buy some things.' I know that would be ridiculous to do. Not only would that be beyond our tight budget, but it would end up being a restaurant that wasn't as nice as the one they went to Saturday night with their dad anyway."

Resist the Temptation

No matter how bad it gets, Fred has to resist the temptation to feel competitive. It would be a no-win situation. No one can really win the heart of a child by purchasing it. It only seems that way for a while. Years later children grow up to resent being bought.

Many times "weekend dads" purchase their children because they don't know what else to do with them. Buying things for the kids is often much easier than actually getting down on the floor and being with them. Other dads find themselves renting a weekend's worth of videos to keep the children busy. Nothing is accomplished under those conditions. The children may initially talk as if they had a wonderful weekend watching television. "It was great, Mom. We watched television all weekend and never had to even make our beds." It won't take long for the children to resent that kind of "entertainment relationship," however.

Wife and Mother Stuck in the Middle

This scenario is also difficult for the Audreys of the world. She is usually dealing with a number of different emotional responses to her ex-husband's purchasing power. Audrey knew it was difficult for Fred that he couldn't spend money like her ex-husband. She began to notice he got irritable every other Sunday evening, before it was time to go pick the children up at the "Big House." She could see that he was feeling insecure. Sundays or Mondays were not good times to talk to Fred about finances.

Aside from having to deal with Fred's feelings of insecurity about the children's Disney World weekends, Audrey had other emotions she had to work through. During the years that she was a single mom her ex-husband kept her on a bare subsistence existence. She had to beg for everything. Now that she was remarried he appeared to have all this extra money hanging around. It sometimes made her quite bitter.

If she wasn't careful she could get very angry about the whole situation. In fact, if Fred and Audrey compared their feelings about this topic, they could easily get the other person fired up. They could fuel each other's anger and that was exactly what they didn't want to do. Sooner or later the anger would spill over onto the children.

Dealing with Misguided Parenting

There was an additional problem for Audrey to consider. Was it good for the children to grow up thinking that they should be given gifts as a token of relationships? She knew the answer was a resounding no, but she didn't know what to do about it. Several times, when she was single, she had asked her ex-husband not to do certain things that she thought were harmful. Her requests were always ignored. Since her marriage to Fred, the gifts to the children had become even more grandiose. Her ex-husband was fearful that he was being replaced, so he was trying to insure his position with the children. He was even more ridiculous about the gifts now that she was married. She was convinced that talking to him about it was a waste of time.

Other things that her former husband did at home were marginal as far as children were concerned. The lack of structure on the weekends meant that they were almost out of control when she got them home. The choice of videos was often just over the line of what she thought to be objectionable for children. But when she tried to talk to her ex-husband he only called her "too religious." The visitation situation was very difficult for her.

It's a Matter of Talking

Audrey and Fred reached the point where they each knew that the other was hurting over the situation. Unfortunately, they felt they couldn't talk to each other about their feelings. Fred, seeing that Audrey was hurting but not talking, thought she wished deep inside that she had stayed married to the better financial provider. He became jealous. Audrey also misinterpreted the situation as she watched Fred keep his pain to himself. She thought that he was probably regretting he had married into this situation.

Each person was hurting emotionally. Each knew the other was also hurting, and yet they couldn't have been more wrong as they tried to interpret the other person's feelings. They were both afraid to talk to the other person because they were fearful that their assumptions were correct. They couldn't have been further from the truth and yet they didn't know it. It was time to talk.

One night it all poured out. In some homes this outpouring of pain might come in the form of an argument, while in others in may come as exhaustion and tears. No matter how the pain erupts, it is important that each parent be prepared to sit and discuss his or her feelings so that the other can learn. The silent treatment tends to make the other person feel as if things are going down the drain—again. Silence can only lead to misinterpretation. When one spouse misreads the other's feelings about the visitation situation, it can cause tremendous problems. In this case Fred was tempted to get into the game of competition. He thought he was losing his stepchildren and his wife. Without talking about it, he was tempted to compete in this ridiculous way.

Audrey was also hurting. "I thought I was losing another marriage," Audrey said in the counseling room. "The way we were venting our hurt at each other made me feel that Fred was giving up. I didn't understand what was going on. I didn't know that I was contributing to his pain."

Talking together about the problem, Audrey and Fred were able to better understand the situation. They could help each other know what the other person was feeling. They could also reassure each other about their love. Audrey was able to help Fred know that the gifts and finances were not something she coveted. As a matter of fact, she strongly disapproved of the whole scenario. "The fact that you spend so much *time* with the children rather than money *on* the children, makes you a much better father, Fred. It only makes me pity their father."

Talking about it, and understanding each other, made the Sunday evening trip to the "Big House" much more palatable. "We used to hate that particular hour," Fred said. "We called it the 'trip to the Big House,' and it was not a term of endearment. It was a label of disgust. Now the label has become something of a joke. I guess what I'm saying is that I'm no longer intimidated by pulling into the driveway. I'm confident in the fact that Audrey loves me." The new confidence was only possible because Audrey and Fred set aside time to talk to each other. They did more than talk. They trusted each other with their feelings.

After You Talk You Must Listen

Many parents would like to tell the children that they can't talk about their weekend with their dad. As tempting as that may be in some cases, it's destructive. The children have had an exciting experience, and they need the opportunity to talk about it with the people they love. It's only natural for them to jump in the car, and want to spill all over about what they've done or received.

The parent needs to do more than just listen, however. A loving parent will set aside a time to let the child talk about the weekend. Perhaps the time could be right after they have been picked up while sitting as a family over a soda. In that setting, eye contact could be such that the children could see they have their mother and stepfather's total attention. The children could also see that it's okay for them to be happy.

Go the Extra Mile

A wise parent and stepparent will do more than just let the child talk about the wonderful things that happened while on visitation. The loving parent will rejoice with the child. If the child was given a new toy, the parent should get excited about that toy and ask to see it or help the child put it together. If the child went someplace special, the parent could let the child tell about it in the most minute detail.

Certainly this seems like going the extra mile. But is it really going out of our way? If a parent really loves the child, shouldn't that parent or stepparent be excited about special things that happen in the child's life—regardless of who gives the child the opportunity?

The child also needs to see that it is okay to like what his dad does for him. Many times children feel as if they must work hard at defending their other parent, because they themselves aren't too sure about that parent. If they work hard at defending him, maybe then other people will think he's special. Mother and Stepparent can give a child a great gift by avoiding anything that would make the child feel that his natural father is less than adequate. Competition will only put the child in the middle of a no-win situation. No matter whose side he takes he loses. Even if one parent is very definitely working at competing for Provider of the Year, don't get drawn into that very destructive role. In fact, to really love the child is to do just the opposite. The extra mile would be for a stepfather to say, "Isn't it great that your father was able to buy that for you? I'm real excited for you, Son. We aren't able to get you things like that, but you know what? It doesn't mean we love you any less. We love you very much!"

Summary

1. Don't get caught competing with an ex-spouse in trying to buy the child.

2. Be careful that the things an ex-spouse does do not cause misunderstandings in your own marriage. Talk about your feelings of inadequacy and failure.

3. Allow the child the opportunity to tell you about all the wonderful things he did over the weekend. Yes, his father was only trying to buy him off with a Disney World Weekend, but the child doesn't know that yet. Let the child share his happiness with you even if you're not the one who provided it for him.

4. Go the extra mile by letting the child know that you're happy for him when he tells about all the things that his other family did.

21 | The Ultimate Blending Glue

My car sits out in the hot South Florida sun every day. One evening as I was leaving my office I got into the car and noticed the rear view mirror lying on the floor. The heat had caused it to come unglued from the windshield—again. This had become a constant problem. I had tried one glue after another and none of them seemed to work. The amazing thing was that each glue was guaranteed to hold that mirror on the windshield for the life of the car. As soon as the heat came, however, the bond fell apart. Once again I was on the hunt for the right glue.

Blending families are on the same quest. What is the element that will keep the family together? Some think the answer is financial. If they can just buy enough things to make everyone happy, the family will do well. It doesn't take long for that myth to be dispelled.

The right neighborhood. The right geographical area of the country. The right schools. An exciting sex life. All these may be significant, but none of these circumstances will supply the gluing element.

The Medallion Ceremony

Elaine and Robert dated for eighteen months and then made the decision to get married and blend their two families. They used a traditional marriage service with the addition of one very significant element: They decided that they wanted to include the children in the actual wedding vows.

Many children fill in as ushers or ring bearers, but in this service the children took part in an exchange—not the exchange of rings, but in an exchange of medallions. The children each received a medallion from their new stepparent.

As the exchange of rings was completed between husband and wife, an exchange of vows and necklaces took place between each stepparent and each child. Each stepparent placed a necklace or gold chain and medallion around the neck of the children of their new spouse. As they did, the parent took a vow before God to love the new spouse and the children, forever. The parent also talked to the child about his or her parental commitment to the family. When this was done there wasn't a dry eye in the building. It was the beginning of the children's learning about the concept of commitment. The medallion was a token for the children to have as a way of remembering the vow their new stepparent had made—a vow to them and a vow before God.

Commitment

The glue that will help the family stick together is the adhesive of commitment. During the early months of the marriage, as the typical disagreements take place, the children are bound to wonder if this relationship will fall apart like the last marriage did. Erin, one of Elaine's daughters, remembers those feelings of insecurity. "When I heard them arguing it scared me. I got that old pain in my stomach. I thought to myself, 'Here we go again.'" This ten-year-old girl was scared to death to get too attached to her new stepdad for fear he wouldn't be around for long. In other words, she wondered if she could risk committing to something that once again might not last.

Slowly each of the children in Elaine and Robert's new family realized something that they weren't accustomed to. No matter how many times this husband and wife disagreed with each other, they were committed to the relationship. The fact that they were committed made it possible to discuss areas of disagreement without fear of divorce. This level of marital commitment gave the children a new sense of security. It allowed them the freedom to learn to accept their new parent without fear of having him vanish from their lives.

One of the greatest gifts parents can give children is this gift of commitment. Children who have had their lives ripped apart by divorce or the death of a parent, have a difficult time understanding the whole idea of commitment. The idea of committing seems to mean that one must open himself up to the pain that could come if the other person were to leave. For many children it seems safer to commit to oneself rather than to a relationship with another person. Due to the scars left by the divorce, some children are frightened of a commitment to a new person.

What a gift it is for children to watch the consistent commitment between their parent and stepparent. As good as this is, and as secure as it will make a child feel, it is still not a permanent glue. Even marital glue can lose its bond.

The Glue That Lasts Forever

One night Erin asked her mother why things were so much better in their home than it had been before. "You and Robert seem so happy together," Erin said. "We've been a family for two years now, and you're still happily married—even when everybody isn't getting along. Is it because you love each other so much?"

Erin asked the million-dollar question and Elaine was ready for it. What her daughter really wanted to know was what kind of glue was making their commitment so lasting. How were they able to weather the many storms that had taken place in their home since the wedding?

"I do love Robert in a very special way, Erin," her mother began. "That's important, but I have learned that it takes more than that. The reason Robert and I are able to get through all that we've gone through is our commitment. Not just our commitment to each other. That's often up and down. It's our commitment to Jesus Christ that has held this family together."

Erin was trying to find the glue that made her mother's marriage seem storm proof. No matter what happened in the relationship her parents seemed to have an understanding that they were going to work through any problem. The key wasn't their own relationship with each other. The glue was their faith in Christ.

I heard a story about a diplomat from South America who was asked why there was such a gap between the development of South America and North America. The reporter continued his question by observing, "Both South America and North America were discovered about the same time and they both had many natural resources. Yet with all those similarities today, North America is industrialized while much of South America is still Third World. What happened?"

Without even hesitating the South American diplomat replied, "The answer to that is easy. South America was discovered in search of gold, but North America was discovered in search of God." The same lesson is true for the marriage.

Children of all ages are searching for something they can commit to—something that will never let them down. Marriages, a mother's health, everything to do with people, will eventually let us down. God, on the other hand, will never let us down. The greatest gift that parents and stepparents can give their children is a philosophy of life that goes beyond circumstances—a faith that children can count on, no matter what happens.

Robert and Elaine were developing a lifestyle that taught their children what real commitment meant. It wasn't in their life or the way they responded to things and people. It was found in a relationship with Jesus Christ. It gave the children a confidence and assurance that they could risk loving other people not only because of who those people are, but also because of Christ. That's the goal.

Elaine and her husband worked on accomplishing that by placing their philosophy of life at the center of the family. They led the children in family devotions on a daily basis. The whole family was involved in an active church. The children were put to bed every night with individual prayers led by a parent. In those prayers each child could see that their parents really did believe in a personal relationship with Christ.

After prayers a parent would always stay in the room with the child for a few minutes. This would give the child an opportunity to ask questions or talk. It was during this bedtime moment that Erin asked why her mother's marriage seemed to be so different this time.

"Mom," Erin went on to ask, "do you ever feel guilty about things you did in your other marriage?"

"I used to, Honey," her mother explained. "I've done a lot of things I wish I could change. I've done a lot of things that I'm not proud of. But Christ died on the cross to forgive my sins, and I've gratefully accepted that gift of forgiveness. Now it's time for me to move on without carrying the weight of that guilt. Now I'm learning to love Christ, and at the same time I'm learning how to love Robert. I can't change the past, but I can change my approach to the present. My commitment is to God. My Lord will never leave me or forsake me."

That and many similar nights, on the side of the bed, were times that little Erin will never forget. They were moments when a mother passed her daughter's hand from the hand of a parent or even a stepfather, into the hand of a Heavenly Father who will never let her down. In this ever-vacillating world, children need to find something they can commit to. The only consistent commitment, the only consistently sticking glue, is a faith in the God who loved us so much that He sent His Son to die for us. Erin learned what to count on to get her through life, because her mother took the time to teach her.

Blending two families is a difficult assignment. Often many couples get bogged down in the process of finding the right glue to bond the new family together. Wise parents will give their children a philosophy of life that reaches far beyond what any human can do. A strong faith in God will be the glue that will help children enter into the stepparent relationship and into future relationships with a healthy attitude. They will be able to grow and commit not because of their confidence in a person they are relating to. They will be able to look past any person's abilities and cling to their faith in Jesus Christ.